THE GRAND CANAL
OF CHINA

South China Morning Post Ltd
New China News Ltd

NEW CHINA NEWS LTD and NEW CHINA PICTURES CO.

Editor-in-Chief: Sun Zhen
Executive Editors: Yue Guofang, Bi Yuenian
Editors: Xie Li, Xu Peide
Special Contributors: Tang Qirang, Zou Yilin, Fei Xin'e
Photographers: Cao Yuquan, Yue Guofang, Zhu Yunfeng, Gao Meiji,
Bi Yuenian, Wu Yuanliu, Xue Tiejun, Lu Quancheng, Ding Jun,
Xu Bang, Li Jilu, Xu Xiaobing, Zhang Zhen, Hua Kangsen,
Mao Mingqing, Huang Jingda, Lu Ke, Yuan Ling, Mao Yongkuan,
Lu Ming, Song Youmin, He Shiyao, Lan Ruxuan, Liu Qingyun
Map Designer: Zhang Peiwen
Cartographer: Zhang Wanhua
Chinese-English Translators: Chen Ruining, Zhang Bihua,
Huang Long, Zhai Shuyao, Song Meiyu, Liu Bingwen, Dai Adi,
Zhang Weimin, Li Lu, Tang Hu
Translation Editors: Huang Long, Chen Ruining, Zhang Bihua,
Zhai Shuyao, Chen Gengtao

SOUTH CHINA MORNING POST LTD
PUBLICATIONS DIVISION

Editor-in-Chief: Howard Coats
Editor: James Kelly
Art Director: Paul Newsham
Designer: Monica Au

Written and compiled by New China News Ltd and
New China Pictures Co.

Edited by South China Morning Post Ltd in conjunction with
New China News Ltd and New China Pictures Co.

Published by the South China Morning Post Publications Division,
Tong Chong Street, Quarry Bay, Hong Kong in co-operation with
New China News Ltd.

Graphic design and presentation by
South China Morning Post Ltd.

Text composition by Filmset Ltd.

Printed by Yee Tin Tong Printing Press Ltd,
Tong Chong Street, Quarry Bay, Hong Kong.

ISBN 962 10 0025 4

Contents

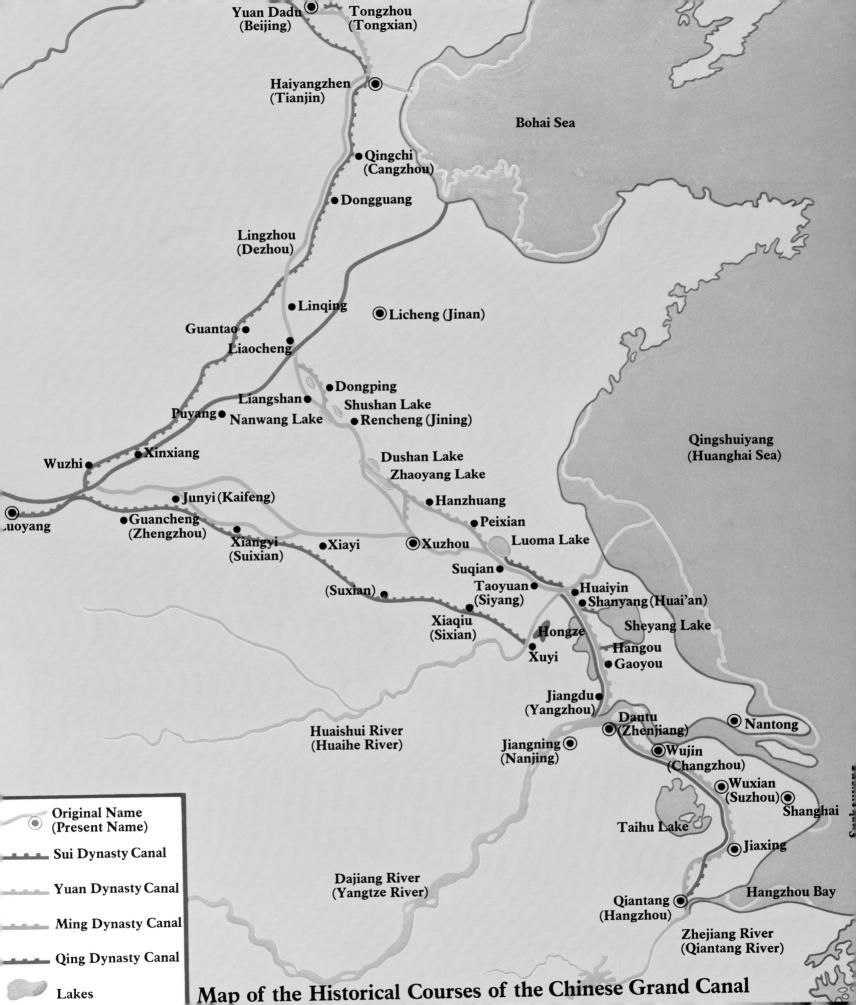

Yuan Dadu
(Beijing)

Tongzhou
(Tongxian)

Haiyangzhen
(Tianjin)

Bohai Sea

Qingchi
(Cangzhou)

Dongguang

Lingzhou
(Dezhou)

Linqing

⊙ Licheng (Jinan)

Guantao

Liaocheng

Dongping

Shushan Lake

Liangshan

Puyang   Nanwang Lake   Rencheng (Jining)

Xinxiang

Dushan Lake

Zhaoyang Lake

Qingshuiyang
(Huanghai Sea)

Wuzhi

Junyi (Kaifeng)

Hanzhuang

Guancheng
(Zhengzhou)

Peixian

Luoyang

Xiangyi
(Suixian)

Xiayi

⊙ Xuzhou

Luoma Lake

Suqian

Taoyuan
(Siyang)

Huaiyin

Shanyang (Huai'an)

(Suxian)

Xiaqiu
(Sixian)

Sheyang Lake

Hongze

Xuyi

Hangou
Gaoyou

Jiangdu
(Yangzhou)

Huaishui River
(Huaihe River)

Dantu
(Zhenjiang)

⊙ Nantong

Jiangning
(Nanjing) ⊙

⊙ Wujin
(Changzhou)

⊙ Wuxian
(Suzhou) ⊙

Shanghai

Taihu Lake

Original Name
(Present Name)

⊙

Sui Dynasty Canal

Jiaxing ⊙

Yuan Dynasty Canal

Dajiang River
(Yangtze River)

Ming Dynasty Canal

Qiantang
(Hangzhou) ⊙

Hangzhou Bay

Qing Dynasty Canal

Zhejiang River
(Qiantang River)

Lakes

Map of the Historical Courses of the Chinese Grand Canal

Foreword

Meandering across the vastness of eastern China, the Grand Canal links up the Yangtze, the Yellow River and three other major waterways. The longest man-made waterway in the world, it is one of the most magnificent navigational and irrigation projects ever built.

Construction of the Grand Canal began 2,400 years ago, but it has been renovated and extended by millions of Chinese over the centuries. It exists as an awesome monument to China's ancient civilisation, a great pioneering undertaking of the working people, and the pride of the Chinese nation.

Stretching across some 2,500 kilometres of a populous area noted for its beautiful landscapes and native products, the Grand Canal since ancient times has played a significant role in transportation and the promotion of cultural and technical exchange between the north and the south. Through the ages artists, scholars and travellers, both Chinese and foreign, have been inspired to produce essays, poems, paintings and stories in its honour.

In the continuing modernisation of their country, the resourceful Chinese are currently emulating the achievements of their forefathers by rebuilding the Grand Canal, on which through navigation has been suspended for a century. The modernisation and reopening of the canal will enable it once more to serve as an artery of north-south water transport. It will not be long before through navigation will resume from the capital of Beijing to the garden city of Hangzhou. The rippling flow of water, the endless stream of ships and the melodious sound of their sirens will all serve to usher in a new era of the Grand Canal.

This book, jointly edited and published by the New China Pictures Company in Beijing, and New China News Ltd and the South China Morning Post Ltd in Hong Kong, carries 362 up-to-date colour photographs along with a text of 35,000 words dealing with the history of the canal, anecdotes and personalities associated with it, and the landscape, customs and products of the regions bordering the canal. It is the first ever album of colour photographs to give a comprehensive and systematic account of the Grand Canal. In the course of editing and publishing the book we received invaluable support and assistance from photographers, geographers, historians, writers, artists and hydraulic engineering experts, to all of whom we express our heartfelt thanks.

Dawn on Weishan Lake in Shandong province. Grand Canal traffic passes through the lake, which was formed in 1194 when the Yellow River overflowed into the channels of the Huai and Sihe rivers.

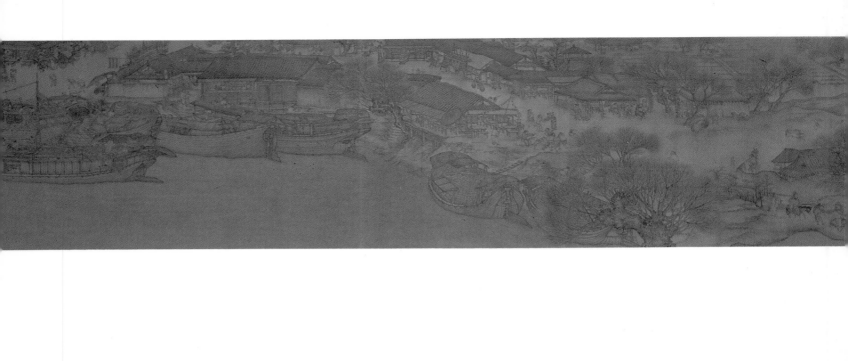

翰林張擇端字正道東武人也幼讀書游
學於京師後習繪事本工其界畫尤嗜於
舟車市橋郭徑別成家數也按向氏評論
圖畫記云西湖爭標圖清明上河圖選入
神品藏者宜寶之大定丙午清明后一日燕
山張著跋

通衢車馬正喧闐祇是
宣和第幾年甫日翰林
呈畫本昇平風物正堪傳

A Wonder of the Ancient World

The Grand Canal ranks with the Great Wall of China, the Pyramids of Egypt and the Buddhagaya Pagoda of India as one of the four great engineering feats of the ancient world. Its length is twenty-two times that of the Panama Canal linking up the Pacific and the Atlantic oceans, and eleven times that of the Suez Canal connecting the Mediterranean with the Red Sea.

Stretching 2,500 kilometres, connecting the vast north of China with the south and crossing ten degrees of latitude, the Grand Canal connects China's five major rivers, the Haihe, the Yellow, the Huaihe, the Yangtze and the Qiantang. As a great man-made waterway, the canal is a lasting symbol of China's ancient civilisation, and an illustrious chapter in the engineering history of the world.

The First Man-Made Waterway

On the map of China one can see that almost all major rivers flow from west to east; only one waterway, the Beijing-Hangzhou Grand Canal, runs from north to south, through the eastern coastal regions.

Before the 5th century B.C., when work on the canal was begun, China had a well-developed east-west transport network, but lacked north-south communications. The middle and lower reaches of the Yellow River, the cradle of the Chinese nation, already had a prosperous economy, advanced production techniques, a dense population and a civilised culture at the time, but the south and north were still backward areas.

During the Shang and Zhou dynasties (from the 11th to 9th centuries B.C.), when the Yellow River valley had entered the Bronze Age, the vast regions in the south and north were still in the Neolithic Age. From the early days, far-sighted emperors became aware of the necessity of building a waterway from north to south to develop the economy and culture of the whole country. On their orders, labourers began work with simple tools to dig crosswise canals linking up the east-west rivers from north to south.

China's earliest man-made waterway, the Hangou Canal linking the Yangtze with the Huaihe River, was built on the orders of King Fuchai of the state of Wu in the Spring and Autumn period (in the 5th century B.C.). The second, the Honggou Canal connecting the Huaihe and Yellow rivers, was dug by Hui Wang, king of the state of Wei in the Warring States period (4th century B.C.). The noted statesman Cao Cao in the Three Kingdoms period (2nd century A.D.) had the Baigou Canal dug to provide a channel between the Yellow and Haihe rivers.

Emperor Yangguang of the Sui dynasty took the project a step further when he ordered a Y-shaped Grand Canal to be built in the 7th century. He set up a comprehensive canal system throughout the country, providing a north-south artery across the five rivers of eastern China.

The Y-shaped canal, centred on Luoyang, then capital of the Sui dynasty in the middle reaches of the Yellow River, ran to Hangzhou in the southeast and Zhuojun (now Beijing) in the northeast. In the 13th century, when the rulers of the Yuan dynasty moved the capital east to Beijing and made it their administrative centre, the Y-shaped canal could no longer meet their requirements.

Ancient Engineering Skills

Kublai Khan, the first emperor of the Yuan dynasty, spent eleven years building the I-shaped Beijing-Hangzhou Grand Canal. This canal, leading south from Beijing, crosses the five rivers and reaches its terminal point, Hangzhou, the capital of Zhejiang province, through the municipality of Tianjin and the provinces of Hebei, Shandong and Jiangsu. It shortened the course from the original 2,500 kilometres to 1,782 kilometres, and became the principal north-south water transport artery.

The north-south Beijing-Hangzhou Canal, completed more than 1,700 years after the original excavation of the Hangou Canal, is a testament to the daring spirit, willpower and wisdom of the Chinese people.

The Grand Canal is divided into seven sections — the Tonghui Canal, the Beiyun Canal, the Nanyun Canal, the Huitong Canal, the Zhongyun Canal, the Liyun Canal and the Jiangnan Canal. It passes through the richly endowed regions of the east China coast and, by dint of the five rivers it crosses, provides water transport for half the country.

If the Suez and Panama canals, built in the late 19th century and the early 20th century respectively, are products of the highly developed hydraulic engineering and

construction technology of modern times, then the Grand Canal is an outstanding example of the hydraulic engineering skills of ancient China.

While the Suez and Panama canals benefited ocean navigation by shortening sea routes of thousands of kilometres to a mere hundred kilometres or so, China's Grand Canal played a quite different role. It expanded the economic and cultural development of an entire civilisation. When huge bulldozers and excavators roared across the construction sites of the Suez and Panama canals, people sensed the awesome power of

中华人民共和国万岁　　　　世界人民大团结万岁

Beijing, capital of the People's Republic of China, and the northern terminus of the Grand Canal.

(Top left) **This 15th century stone figure at Linqing was a gift from the emperor on the occasion of the opening of the Huitong Canal.**

(Left) **The meeting place of the Beiyun and Nanyun canals, at the Hongqiao Bridge in the city of Tianjin.**

modern machinery. But how much more extraordinary were the achievements, more than 1,300 years earlier, of a million labourers working in coordination, with primitive tools, to dig a canal five hundred kilometres in length!

The Suez and Panama canals, which have had a great influence on world shipping, boast only six sluice gates, but one 100-kilometre section of the Grand Canal — the "Sluice-gate Canal" — has well over sixty sluice gates to deal with its complex topography. Moreover, only thirty-odd bridges span the Suez and Panama canals, but more than 3,000 bridges cross the main channel of the southern section of the Grand Canal, which passes through a region criss-crossed by a network of small rivers. If all bridges spanning the tributaries are counted, the total number exceeds 12,000. The Grand

Canal has more sluice gates and bridges than any other waterway in the world.

The construction of the sluice gates, the principal means of controlling water flow to ensure navigation, shows that ancient China already had the knowhow to construct man-made canals under very difficult topographical conditions. For instance, it should have been impossible to dig the canal through Shandong province with its rolling hills and shortage of water sources, but the technicians of the time succeeded in diverting river water from afar and retaining it stage by stage by the use of sluice gates. The numerous bridges also demonstrate that ancient China had solved the problem of developing both water and land traffic in areas criss-crossed by rivers and streams, and had gained experience in joint water-land transport.

13

(Left) A busy scene on the canal.

(Right) Relics of shovels and picks used to dig the canal in the Song dynasty (960-1279).

(Extreme right) An old canal boatman at the helm of his craft.

(Below) The canal passes through a network of rivers and lakes.

In the 14th and 15th centuries, when hydraulic engineering and navigational management were still in an embryonic stage throughout the world, China had already reached a high level in applying those theories to canal construction and navigational management. The remains of many water control projects and navigation facilities along the canal, some of them still very well preserved, are today proving valuable aids in the study of the hydraulic engineering and inland river navigation management of ancient China.

The Canal's Historical Role

The Grand Canal, which has been open to navigation in whole or in part for nearly 2,000 years, has played a significant role in Chinese history. With its low cost and large volume of freight, the canal has played a large part in developing communications between the north and the south.

It helped to spread advanced technology and cultural development along the Yellow River valley to the south in ancient times, and large numbers of people moved to settle in the south by way of the canal.

Agricultural production in the richly endowed Jiangsu and Zhejiang provinces south of the Yangtze developed rapidly with the advent of the canal. During the Qin and Western Han dynasties before the 1st century A.D., the imperial court imported grain mainly from Henan, Hebei and Shandong provinces along the middle and lower reaches of the Yellow River, but after the 7th century rulers of the Tang and Northern Song dynasties depended largely on regions south of the Yangtze for their grain supply. They shipped more than 300,000 tons of grain annually to the north via the canal. Jiangsu and Zhejiang became the most economically advanced regions in China after the 12th century. It was mainly from

southern China that rulers of the Yuan, Ming and Qing dynasties (from the 13th to the 19th century) got their grain, financial income and manpower for the military and civil services.

The emperor and the royal family depended on the vast region south of the Yangtze for the supply of tea, sugar, fruits, silk, paper, writing brushes and inkstones, building materials, pearls, hawksbill turtles, jadeite, flowers, grasses, woods and stones. Tens of thousands of ships shuttled along the canal every year to transport the goods, and some 120,000 soldiers were used as seamen to ship grain north to the capital. The Beijing-Hangzhou Canal became a lifeline for the imperial courts. For that reason the emperors of the Yuan, Ming and Qing dynasties spared neither labour nor material to ensure its smooth operation.

Wherever the canal extended, the area's economy developed rapidly, and industrial and commercial centres sprang up. Among the most notable cities were Hangzhou, Jiaxing, Suzhou, Zhenjiang, Yangzhou, Huai'an, Huaiyin, Jining, Linqing and Dezhou. They became important grain shipping ports, and key trading centres between the north and south. Merchants from all over the country and from other countries in Southeast Asia and the Middle East did business there.

Huaiyin, Linqing and Dezhou were communications hubs between nine provinces, and goods were sent to them from all areas of the country via the five rivers connected by the canal. On sale in their markets were furs from northeast China and fruits and medicinal herbs from southwest China's Sichuan and Guangdong provinces. Linqing, a small town which came into existence with the digging of the Shandong section of the canal, soon developed into a city with a population of around 800,000.

The growth of these cities promoted the rapid expansion of handicraft arts and agriculture along the canal. The silk production centres moved from the north to the south with the digging of the canal. Large stretches of mulberry fields were opened along the canal south of the Yangtze, and virtually every family in city and countryside alike went in for silkworm breeding and silk weaving. As the home of tea, China produced most of its famous tea varieties in regions bordering the canal.

Yixing ceramic pots are loaded on to barges for shipment to other parts of China.

(Left) Dilapidated houses at an ancient canal port in Zhenjiang, Jiangsu province.

(Top right) Fields in blossom bring a blaze of colour to the banks of the canal in southern China.

(Right) Dusk on a waterway in beautiful Suzhou, Jiangsu province.

16

The Grand Canal also helped to spread the splendid culture of ancient China. The civilisation of the north began to spread to the Yangtze valley soon after Hangou and Honggou, the two earliest sections of the canal, were dug. In the 1st century A.D., the city of Yangzhou by the Yangtze became the cultural centre of the south. With the completion of the Sui dynasty canal in the early 7th century, culture spread southwards through the canal. Many poets, writers and artists of the late Tang dynasty moved to the south in the 9th century, and Hangzhou,

Suzhou, Yangzhou and Huai'an grew into famous cultural centres with a galaxy of talent. Prominent men of letters such as Lu Guimeng and Pi Rixiu grew up in Suzhou.

By the 12th century, almost all of the famous men of letters were from the south. More novels, poems and other literary works were created with the development of printing and publishing in the south. Southern culture began to excel that of the north. Many public and private schools were set up in Jiangsu and Zhejiang provinces during the Yuan, Ming and Qing dynasties, and culture spread extensively in cities and countryside. The philosophy, literature, science and art of ancient China flourished, and many noted scholars came to the fore. Fine arts and handicraft art flourished. Masterpieces of embroidery, clay sculpture, carving and lacquerwork appeared in the south, and large numbers of art treasures were created.

Age-old Enchantment

The Grand Canal has enthralled travellers through the ages with the scenic spots and places of historical interest along its banks. A journey along it takes the visitor past picturesque mountains and lakes and

oriental-style gardens, and allows him to taste delicious Chinese food and famous local products and enjoy the distinctive local flavours north and south of the Yangtze.

Noted poets, writers and artists throughout Chinese history gathered or settled in the major cities along the canal, leaving behind them innumerable works of art and literature.

The well-known poets Li Bai and Du Fu of the Tang dynasty (8th century) did a lot of travelling along the canal. Li Bai even moved his residence to Jining. The poet Bai Juyi of the late Tang dynasty (10th century) and the literary giant Su Dongpo of the Northern Song dynasty (12th century) were responsible for two famous beauty spots, the Bai Causeway and the Su Causeway, on the West Lake in Hangzhou, the southern terminal of the canal.

High officials and noble lords, gentry, celebrities and rich merchants, wielding their power and influence, travelled from place to place along the canal and indulged in lives of opulent extravagance. One rich merchant spent an enormous sum of money to gather together all the famous dishes from throughout the country for a banquet, and spent several thousand ounces of silver to build a villa.

Emperors of all the dynasties in history used the Grand Canal as an "imperial canal". When the Sui Dynasty canal was opened, the first travellers were the Emperor Yangguang together with his empress, concubines and high-ranking officials. Riding in a huge "dragon boat" more than thirteen metres long and six metres high with a carrying capacity of several hundred people, the emperor made his way from the

A bargee and his family on the canal. The couple's forefathers were all boatmen who spent their lives shipping grain to the imperial capitals.

(Left) The Bell Tower and the Drum Tower by the side of Shisha Lake in Beijing. In the 13th and 14th centuries this was the site of Jishuitan Wharf, the capital's oldest commercial district.

(Right) The Grand Canal is still serving its primary function as a means of shipping grain throughout eastern China.

19

capital at Luoyang to Yangzhou in the south. Dou Hou, wife of the Emperor Gao Zong of the Tang dynasty, visited Zhejiang via the canal. Emperors Yongle and Zheng De of the Ming dynasty and emperors Kangxi and Qianlong of the Qing dynasty also made inspection tours of the south by way of the canal.

In medieval times, foreign envoys, travellers, monks and priests, scholars and even visiting foreign monarchs chose to travel north in luxury along the canal to the Chinese capital. Western-style restaurants and hotels, shops and interpreter services were at that time available in the major cities along the canal. Marco Polo and other noted travellers from Italy travelled along it many times.

They described Suzhou and Hangzhou, the two most scenic spots along the canal, as "the most beautiful and magnificent cities in the world". Later came businessmen and imams from Morocco and Egypt, and merchants from Japan and India. In the 15th century Paduka Pahala, the Sultan of Sulu in the Philippines, travelled to Beijing by way of the canal with his wife and officials.

From the 18th century on, foreign missionaries, merchants and scholars frequently toured the canal.

The Decline of the Grand Canal

The age-old Grand Canal, which had done so much to spread the highly-developed ancient economy and culture of the Yellow River basin to China's north and south, eventually fell victim to natural disaster. The Yellow River contains an average of 37.6 kilograms of silt per cubic metre of water, the highest concentration in the world. It has overflowed its banks, breached its dykes and changed its course many times over the centuries.

When it ran rampant in 1127, it took over the estuary of the Huaihe River in northern Jiangsu province as its own sea outlet, resulting in the backward flow of the Huaihe flood into the canal. The great volume of silt from the Yellow River raised the canal bed in northern Jiangsu, impeding north-south transport, and turned Hongze Lake, the biggest lake along the canal, into a "suspension lake" whose bed was six to seven metres higher than the land.

(Right) This dugout canoe was unearthed in 1960 from the site of an ancient ferry at Guangzhou. It was chiselled out of one big *nanmu* tree, and is 13.65 metres long.

(Left) A peaceful rural scene on the banks of the canal.

(Below) The village store stocks a variety of merchandise.

A flood in the 16th century breached the lake dyke and inundated a nearby town. In 1855 the Yellow River overflowed its banks. The flood blocked a section of the canal in Shandong province and silted up the 100-kilometre-long channel.

Before the Qing imperial court could finish the repairs the river ran wild again. As the corrupt and incompetent Qing officials watched helplessly, through navigation along the canal came to a halt. As a result, industry and commerce in the many cities by the canal declined sharply.

In the periods of the civil wars among the warlords and the rule of the Kuomintang regime before the late 1940s, the Grand Canal suffered from neglect for many years, and fell into a state of disrepair.

Dawn of a New Era

On its founding in 1949, People's China began large-scale renovation of the dilapidated ancient canal. Navigable sections in northern Jiangsu and in areas south of the Yangtze were thoroughly dredged. The government built new sluice gates or rebuilt old ones, repaired the long dykes along the waterway and reopened the silted-up estuary of the Huaihe River, relieving the threat of flood from the Huaihe. At the spot where the canal meets the Yellow River, solid dykes and huge flood-control sluices were built to prevent the Yellow River silt from flowing into the canal.

The people's government appropriated special funds to renovate major lakes along the canal so that they could again serve as "water tanks" for flood storage and detention to regulate the water level of the navigable channels. A comprehensive project to harness Hongze Lake was completed, in view of the fact that the lake, with its 1,000-square-kilometre water surface, receives annually more than 100,000 million cubic metres of floodwater from three provinces in the north, west and south and has a great bearing on canal navigation.

In 1958 about 1.3 million labourers were organised to dig the 183-kilometre-long "Northern Jiangsu Trunk Ditch" and construct a high-power irrigation and drainage pumping station. The projects were completed in eighty-three days. As a result, the "suspension lake" Hongze can now regulate the water level of the Grand Canal and drain off floodwater directly into the sea in high

21

water seasons. The lake water is also used to generate power and irrigate about 677,000 hectares of land, thus creating new "granaries" of the areas along the canal section which were under constant flood menace for nearly a thousand years.

The section of the canal from Hanxian county in northern Jiangsu to Hangzhou has again been opened to traffic all year round, restoring the water-land transport network along a thousand-kilometre-long route together with the rail and road lines.

China has started a bold new scheme to divert water to the arid north from the rainy south in the 1980s. Beginning in 1985, the Yangtze water will flow to Beijing and Tianjin via the Grand Canal at a capacity of 100 cubic metres per second.

Some 240,000 people took part in the project to widen and deepen the Liyunhe Canal in 1982. Dredging is due to start soon on the Huitong, Nanyun, Beiyun and Tonghui canals.

The ancient Grand Canal will shortly rediscover its former glory, serving as a north-south shipping artery along with the Beijing-Hangzhou Railway and coastal shipping routes. It will last forever as a symbol of Chinese inventiveness and resourcefulness.

The picturesque West Lake in Hangzhou, southern terminus of the Grand Canal.

(Left) The canal also serves as a source of food, as this fisherman empties his net by the light of the setting sun.

(Right) Seven-masted fishing boats have plied the waters of Lake Taihu for the past 800 years.

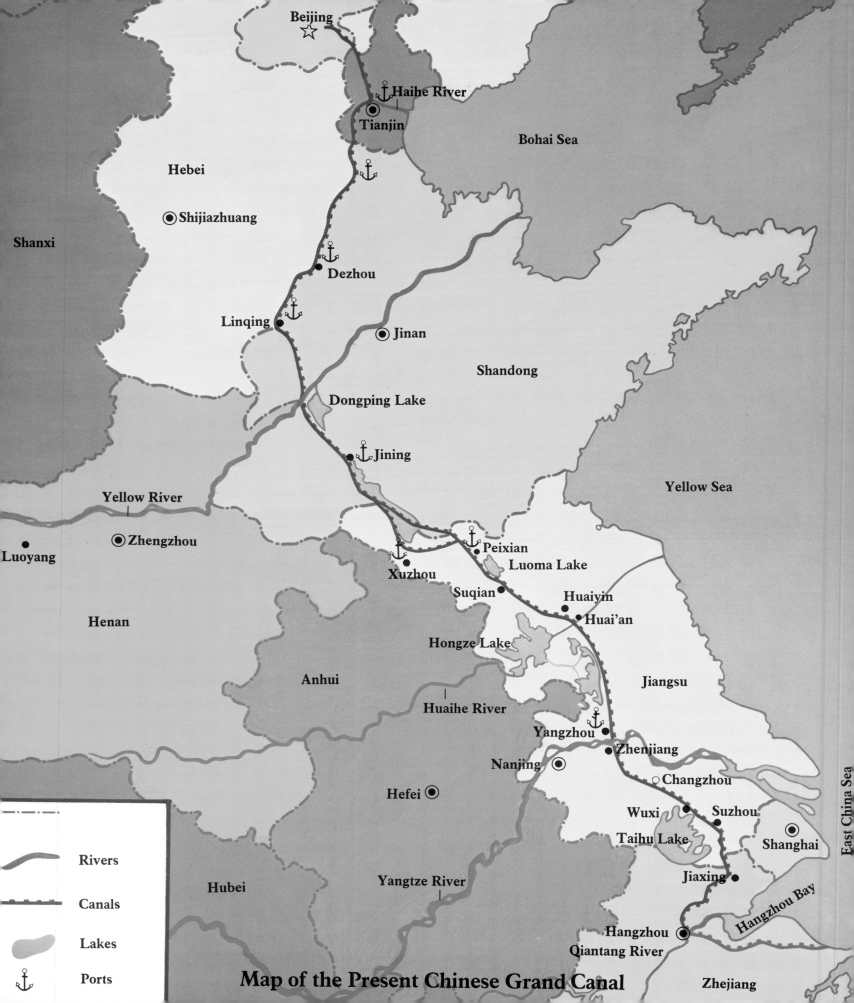

Map of the Present Chinese Grand Canal

Beijing

Haihe River

Tianjin

Hebei

Bohai Sea

Shijiazhuang

Shanxi

Dezhou

Linqing

Jinan

Shandong

Dongping Lake

Yellow Sea

Jining

Yellow River

Zhengzhou

Luoyang

Xuzhou

Peixian

Luoma Lake

Suqian

Huaiyin

Huai'an

Henan

Hongze Lake

Anhui

Jiangsu

Huaihe River

Yangzhou

Zhenjiang

Nanjing

Changzhou

Hefei

Wuxi

Suzhou

Taihu Lake

Shanghai

East China Sea

Yangtze River

Jiaxing

Hubei

Hangzhou Bay

Rivers

Canals

Lakes

Ports

Hangzhou

Qiantang River

Zhejiang

The Seven Sections of the Canal

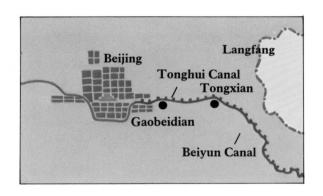

Tonghui Canal

Tonghui Canal, once the northernmost section of the Beijing-Hangzhou Grand Canal, occupies a position of particular importance in the history of Chinese hydraulic engineering as a difficult project built with high-level construction techniques. It was the last section of the canal to be completed, but its life was to be a short one.

During the reign of Kublai Khan, the first emperor of the Yuan dynasty in the second half of the 13th century, the court received 816,000 tons of grain every year from all parts of the country, 537,000 tons of which were transported to Dadu (Beijing) from the south. However, when the grain was shipped either by sea or via the canal to Tongxian county, twenty kilometres east of the capital, it had to be carried on to Dadu overland — a costly business which caused heavy losses among the draught animals. In 1276 the Prime Minister, Bo Yan, recommended that Guo Shoujing, an expert in hydraulic engineering, be given charge of the renovation of the Grand Canal and the opening of a new section from Dadu to Tongxian county to allow the grain to be shipped directly to the capital.

Guo Shoujing investigated and surveyed all aspects of the water sources and terrain of Dadu. At the foot of Shenshan Hill (now Fenghuang Hill in Changping county of the Beijing Municipality) northwest of Dadu he discovered Baifu Spring, a constant supply of water. He decided to build an embankment there to lead the water down the hill. In 1293 Kublai Khan called out more than 20,000 soldiers and craftsmen to build the project, and ordered all officials from the Prime Minister down to take part in the construction.

The builders first constructed Baifu embankment around the spring, which had a higher elevation than Dadu, then channelled water from all the springs nearby into a single 25-kilometre course and led it to Wengshan Lake (now Kunming Lake in the Summer Palace). This was the famous Baifu-Wengshan Ditch. It was then connected with the Gaoliang River (or Zhahe River) in Dadu, and water was diverted from the ditch to Jishuitan Lake (now Shishahai Lake in Beijing) and then to the Luhe River (now Beiyun Canal) in Tongxian county. The total length of the canal was 77.7 kilometres.

As the city of Beijing was more than twenty metres higher than Tongxian county, the bed of the Tonghui Canal sloped downhill and the water flowed rapidly. This would have made it very difficult for grain carriers to sail against the current from south to north, so Guo Shoujing had sluice gates and ship locks built at intervals of every five kilometres to regulate the volume of water. In building the sluice gates, he invented the technique of driving wooden piles in as a foundation, and paving the top with stone slabs.

After the Tonghui Canal was completed in 1293, boats carrying grain from the south could sail directly to the wharf of Jishuitan Lake in Dadu. When Kublai Khan passed through Jishuitan on his way home from Shangdu (now Dolonnur in Inner

(Top left) **Shishahai Lake, which in the Yuan dynasty was the Tonghui Canal's busy Jishuitan port, is now one of the largest skating rinks in Beijing.**

(Centre left) **Gaoliang River, once part of the Tonghui Canal, flows through Zizhuyuan (Purple Bamboo) Park in Beijing.**

(Bottom left) **Bali (Eight Li) Bridge, built in 1449 during the Ming dynasty, is four kilometres from Tongxian county and the oldest construction on the Tonghui Canal.**

(Below) **Fuquan Spring in Changping county, the main water source of the Tonghui Canal.**

Mongolia), he was so gladdened by the sight of so many ships, high piles of grain and hawking pedlars that he named this section "Tonghui (Through and Beneficial) Canal".

But the heyday of the canal was to be a brief one. Constant mountain torrents destroyed the water diversion works, and water frequently ran short. In 1369, the fortunes of the Tonghui Canal declined along with those of the Yuan dynasty.

In the early days of the Ming dynasty the capital was rebuilt and all the courses of the canal in Beijing were incorporated into the imperial city. The Changping area in the upper reaches of the canal was selected as the site for the imperial tombs (the thirteen Ming Tombs), thus cutting off the main water source of the Tonghui Canal. During

the next 200 years the Ming court tried several times to reopen the old courses of the canal, but failed for lack of water sources. So what is today known as the Beijing-Hangzhou Grand Canal in fact reaches Tongxian county only.

The old Tonghui Canal, running between Beijing and Tongxian county, later became a tributary of the Beiyun Canal. The old channels of the Baifu-Wengshan Ditch are now used as ditches of the Beijing-Miyun Canal — the water supply lifeline of the Chinese capital. The small Gaoliang River running quietly behind the well-known Zizhuyuan Park, once a part of the Tonghui Canal, now winds past Baishiqiao (White Stone Bridge) and the Beijing Exhibition Hall, and flows into Jishuitan Park.

Beiyun Canal

Beiyun Canal, or northern canal, is the 155-kilometre section of the Grand Canal running from Tongxian county to the city of Tianjin, most of it along the old canal channels of the Ming and Qing dynasties.

Known as Tongzhou Grain Transport River in the Yuan dynasty (1271-1368), it was an important section of the grain route from the south to the capital. In the time of Emperor Yongle of the Ming dynasty, wharves were built at intervals of nine kilometres all along it. Hundreds of vessels laden with articles of tribute to the imperial court and goods for trade, carrying officials, merchants and other passengers bound for the capital, were a constant sight at the wharves.

Official boats were separated into groups known as "*bang*" in the Qing dynasty. A *bang* consisted of fifty boats, each with a complement of twenty-six sailors under the supervision of a petty officer. A wharf accommodated at most eighty-eight *bang* a day. Fleets of large grain carriers, each sixty metres long, appeared in the late Qing dynasty. Anchored in the wharf, a grain fleet stretched for more than one kilometre from its head to its tail. When it weighed anchor, the captain had to beat a large bronze gong for one hour to transmit the order down the line.

Navigability on the Beiyun Canal was an off and on affair over the years. Crossing the arid, water-deficient Beijing-Tianjin area, there was a drop of more than 20 metres from its upper to its lower reaches. In dry seasons grain ships from the south had great

(Left) **The Ming Tombs reservoir, source of the Beiyun Canal.**

(Right) **A portrait of Emperor Kangxi of the Qing dynasty, who made surveys of the Kuangergang Spillway Dam and other irrigation projects on the Beiyun Canal.**

(Below) **Ruins of the Kuangergang Spillway Dam, built in 1700.**

difficulty sailing against the current. And in high water seasons it often overflowed its banks. In the Ming dynasty this section of the canal was put under military protection. Canal guards, wearing sleeveless jackets with the word "guard" on them, were stationed every two kilometres along the embankment to patrol the canal, inspect its dangerous sections and take strict precautions against any attempts to breach the dykes and divert the water for illegal use.

In the 120 years of their rule, Emperor Kangxi (1662-1723) and his grandson, Emperor Qianlong (1736-1796), regarding the Beiyun Canal as the last important link in the safe transport of grain to the capital, went to great pains to have it renovated. When the dykes around Kuangergang in its middle reaches were breached twice, in 1697 and 1699, Emperor Kangxi personally surveyed the dangerous section and inspected the effects of the disasters. He allocated a million ounces (about 32,000 kilograms) of silver to build up the Kuangergang Spillway Dam, which was later hailed as the "dragon back" of the Beiyun Canal. By the side of

Farmers sell rush baskets and other local handicrafts at a country fair on the canal banks.

(Top left) Remains of the ancient canal banks at the town of Hexiwu, Tianjin. Hexiwu, which was destroyed in a flood in 1669, was known as the "throat" of the Beiyun Canal.

(Left) Qu Zeshan (right), 72, a descendant of canal guards of the Qing dynasty, has been a canal bank patrolman for thirty years.

(Extreme left) A stone tablet which was set up when Emperor Qianlong reconstructed the Kuangergang Spillway Dam.

(Following page) The Beiyun Canal cuts through the ancient town of Yangcun.

the dam an imperial tablet bearing the words *Daoliujiyun* (Divert-Water-To-Canal) was erected.

According to historical records, the dam, 192 metres long and thirty metres wide, had more than 2,000 cypress piles driven into its foundations. The top was paved with five layers of thirty-centimetre-thick packed earth (building material composed of thirty percent clay and seventy percent lime mixed with glutinous rice water), two layers of two-metre-long and thirty-centimetre-wide rectangular slabs of granite, and then a thick layer of surface earth.

Beiyun Canal has been comprehensively renovated since 1949. Its 21-kilometre channel through Tongxian has been straightened, the banks laid with stones, and in 1973 ten sluice gates were constructed. Water diverted from the canal has been used to irrigate around 67,000 hectares of farmland criss-crossed by a network of ditches. This has been an enormous boon to local agricultural production.

A sixteen-way flood-diversion sluice has been built on the site of the old dam at Kuangergang, and the old eight-way sluice constructed in 1934 has been rebuilt into an eleven-way one to form a cluster of sluices. A number of historical relics, including broken ship planks and porcelain plates, were unearthed in the course of the construction. According to archaeologists, they were the wreckage of a fleet that capsized in a flood.

Another dam at Qujiadian, fifteen kilometres from the city of Tianjin, built in 1932 as the first major dam in north China, has now been replaced with an eleven-way check gate completed in 1969. Water flows at a volume of 1,020 cubic metres per second through the new gate, the largest on the Beiyun Canal. Near it is another cluster comprising a six-way diversion sluice, a ship lock and other gates. In the early days after the completion of the gates, wooden boats with a deadweight of ten tons could sail between Qujiadian and Kuangergang in high water seasons. But as the water source gradually dried up, shipping was suspended. Beiyun Canal has now become the main water conduit from the Miyun Reservoir to Tianjin, though water in its upper reaches is still used to irrigate farmland.

34

(Top left) **The tranquil old course of the Beiyun Canal.**

(Bottom left) **A millstone-like dam on the Beiyun Canal built with piles of limestone rocks in the fashion of ancient anti-flood measures.**

(Right) **A threshing ground by the Qujiadian check gate near Tianjin.**

(Below) **Jingang Bridge in Tianjin, where the Beiyun Canal joins the Haihe River.**

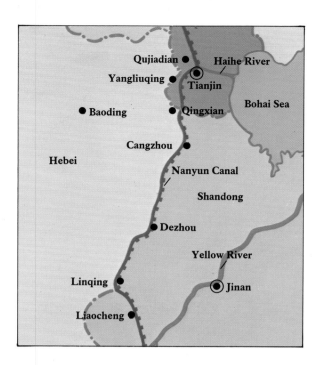

Nanyun Canal

The 542-kilometre stretch running from the north China port of Tianjin to Linqing in Shandong province is the longest section of the Grand Canal. The Nanyun Canal, north of the Yellow River, was dug in A.D. 204 during the reign of Emperor Jianan of the Eastern Han Dynasty when Cao Cao, one of the best-known statesmen of ancient China, was in power.

The Nanyun Canal begins on the western outskirts of Tianjin and stretches south to Yangliuqing, where an intricate network of ditches drains off the canal water to irrigate a large rice-growing area. The rice here grows so luxuriantly that it has come to be known as the "Yangtze Valley" of the north China plain. The popular Xiaozhan variety of paddy rice is grown here.

From Yangliuqing the canal continues to the town of Duliu at the confluence of the Ziya and Daqing rivers. In the 15th century (Ming dynasty) a waterway named after the town was built to divert floodwater to the Bohai Gulf. This freed the area from flooding, which also threatened shipping on the Grand Canal. Between the Duliu River and Cangzhou lie lowlands where floodwater tends to accumulate.

During the reign of Emperor Yongle of

The Nanyun Canal running south from Tianjin.

(Top right) Chen Rui, 102, (right) worked as a child with his father on the barges transporting grain to Beijing. He also helped to dredge the Nanyun Canal.

(Right) A newly-built pumping station on the site of the old Ming dynasty Jiamaying control lock. The Nanyun Canal supplies water to the surrounding countryside and cities.

(Left) The Sinusi Water Control Project — the largest of its kind on the Nanyun Canal — diverts Yellow River water to the Grand Canal.

the Ming dynasty, Song Li, the Minister of Communications, ordered the building of three canals to divert floodwater from an eighty-kilometre section of the Grand Canal and make it safer for shipping.

Cangxian county (present-day Cangzhou) was in ancient times a popular place of banishment. Lin Cong, a martial arts instructor of Emperor Huizong's imperial guards in the Northern Song dynasty, was only one of the many exiled here. Historical relics have been found which can be traced back to the time Lin Cong joined the peasants' uprising in Mount Liangshan.

Further south, the Nanyun Canal enters Shandong province's Dezhou City, a water transport hub and gateway to the ancient capital. A project was launched here in the Ming and Qing dynasties to regulate the level of the Grand Canal by channelling water either to or from the Zhanghe River.

But as the river was heavily silt-laden, dredging operations had to be carried out each year. In the reign of Emperor Kangxi of the Qing dynasty in the 17th century, maintenance stations were set up on both banks of the canal to ensure smooth navigation. Whenever ships ran aground, workers from the stations were sent to dredge the canal.

A number of conservation projects were undertaken to de-silt the canal in ancient times. One project built during the reign of Yongle in the Ming dynasty worked quite well by creating a swift flow of floodwater to churn up and carry away the silt.

To make more water available for Tianjin, the government has in the past few years started a new project to channel water from the Yellow River to supply the four million residents as well as the factories of the port city.

A sketch map of the Sinusi Water Control Project.

(Top right) **A stone tablet from the flood-submerged Dawangmiao dredging house in the Ming and Qing dynasties. Some 320 dredgers were housed there.**

(Right) **Labourers excavate the Nanyun Canal in 1971 to divert water from the Yellow River.**

(Left) **The Dezhou Ship Lock, rebuilt in the 1950s on the site of the old Qing dynasty lock, and no longer in use since the suspension of shipping on the Nanyun Canal.**

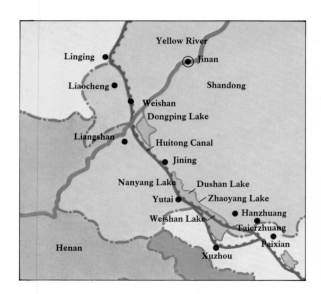

Huitong Canal

The Huitong Canal in Shandong province is regarded as the heart of the Grand Canal, because its completion provided the final link in the canal as a through waterway, and its silting-up led to the 19th century suspension of navigation.

In the early period of the Yuan dynasty (1271-1368), the grain route from south to north China took a meandering path along the Y-shaped waterway from northern Jiangsu province to Henan, switched over to land transport for the journey to Linqing in Shandong province, and then turned north via the Grand Canal. Transport on this roundabout water-land route, 600 kilometres long, was expensive and time-consuming, and boats had to sail against the current. Kublai Khan, the first emperor of the Yuan dynasty, decided to dig a new canal through Shandong province to form an I-shaped waterway that cut the route by 300 kilometres. In 1276, the thirteenth year of his reign, he appointed his defence minister to take charge of the project.

Excavation of the Huitong Canal was started in 1289 following the opening of the Jizhou Canal. It took thirty-six years to remove the huge volume of earth and stones and build the network of navigation facilities on the two canals. Meanwhile the Tonghui Canal from Tongzhou to Beijing was also opened to traffic. This meant that foodgrains from south China could then be shipped directly to Beijing from Hangzhou, Suzhou and other cities.

A silted-up, reed-strewn section of the Huitong Canal.

(Top left) This decorated archway bears an inscription by Kublai Khan, first emperor of the Yuan dynasty, to mark the opening of the Huitong Canal to shipping.

(Left) The starting point of the Huitong Canal.

(Top right) A Song dynasty stele unearthed in the digging of the Huitong Canal. The two characters Bao Zang (precious deposits) engraved on it were written by the famous calligrapher Mi Fu.

(Right) The Liaocheng Water Control Project, used to divert water from the Huitong Canal, the Yellow River and the Haihe River for transportation and irrigation.

The Grand Canal was complete, and Kublai Khan was so pleased that he personally gave the final section the name Hui-Tong-He, meaning "canal linking up all sections". Once the Huitong Canal was open to navigation the Grand Canal became "a dragon's rein" in the hands of the emperors of all the dynasties to follow, giving them absolute control of water transportation.

The construction of the Huitong Canal was an indication of the high level ancient China had attained in hydraulic engineering science. Shandong province was just about the last place one would choose to dig a canal, because of its complicated topography and shortage of water sources. But the Chinese engineers and technicians successfully overcame the problems by building a complicated series of locks and dams to divert water from a river with a higher level. In 1411, on orders from Emperor Chengzhu of the Ming dynasty (1368-1644), the Shandong section was dredged on a large scale to allow in more water, facilities were added and navigation improved.

The most famous project on the canal was the Nanwang Bifurcation Gate, built in the early 15th century. Surveyed and designed by an aged peasant expert named Bai Ying and completed under the guidance of Song Li, Minister of Communications, the project

(Left) **The Shan-Sha'an Hall on the banks of the Huitong Canal, built as a lodging house by merchants from Shanxi and Sha'anxi provinces in the 17th century, when Grand Canal traffic was at its heaviest.**

(Right) **Linqing's Huitong Bridge, built in the Ming dynasty on the site of a collapsed sluice gate.**

(Bottom right) **Guangyue Drum Tower, which once beat out time signals to travellers on the canal.**

(Below) **The scenic Dragon Hill in Linqing, 100 metres high, formed from earth excavated from the canal in the Yuan and Ming dynasties.**

included water diversion gates, a ship lock and a long dyke against the Yellow River's flood. Some 200 years after its completion, when Emperor Kangxi of the Qing dynasty (1644-1911) came to the area on an inspection tour, he hailed Bai Ying as an ingenious waterworks expert. Latter-day visitors have been no less impressed. One American hydraulic engineer who saw the project in the early part of this century pronounced himself astounded that such an accurate calculation of engineering data could have been made and such a scientific and highly efficient project conceived in the 14th-15th centuries, when hydraulic engineering was a primitive science and modern instruments and geological data were non-existent.

The Huitong Canal runs through the two ancient "civilisation states" of Qi and Lu. It flows past Mount Tai, one of China's five famous mountains, and Qufu, the home town of Confucius, the renowned Chinese educator and thinker.

It was customary for emperors of the feudal dynasties to go ashore at ports on the Huitong Canal and switch to carriages or horseback for trips to Qufu or Mount Tai. Li Bai, a well-known Tang dynasty poet, lived in the Taibai House on the banks of the canal for twenty-three years. Liangshan, the scene of the peasant uprising in the Northern Song dynasty depicted in the classical

Chinese novel *The Water Margin,* was located at the southern end of the Huitong Canal. Dongping Lake, now a reservoir of the Huitong Canal, was then a part of the main channel. The tomb of Paduka Pahala, the Sultan of Sulu (now part of the Philippines) is in the city of Dezhou by the Huitong Canal.

In 1855 (the fifth year of the reign of Emperor Xianfeng of the Qing dynasty) the Yellow River burst its banks at Tongwaxiang, in Henan province, and changed its outlet to the sea from north Jiangsu province to Lijin in Shandong province. The flood cut through the Huitong Canal, and most of its bed was silted up and became flat land. Navigation on the Grand Canal came to a halt.

Today, with the development of the national economy, the government plans to reopen the Huitong Canal and restore it to its former glory.

The Huitong Canal crosses north China's cotton belt, where descendants of canal boatmen have become skilled cotton growers.

(Right) **Anshan, an important port at the end of the Jizhou Canal from the 13th to the 19th century.**

(Top left) **Seasonal navigation continues on the Jizhou Canal between Jining and Taierzhuang. Outside Jining is the widest part of the canal.**

(Centre left) **The only remaining embankment of the old Huitong Canal after the Yellow River flood cut the canal in two in 1855.**

(Bottom left) **The Nanwang Bifurcation Project on the Jizhou Canal, a watershed between the northern and southern sections of the Grand Canal.**

(Extreme left) **The Water Taming Iron Tower on the banks of the Huitong Canal.**

Jizhou Canal

The Jizhou Canal was dug on the orders of Kublai Khan, the first emperor of the Yuan dynasty, as a first step in the creation of the north-south Grand Canal. Its construction started in 1276 under the guidance of the then Minister of Defence, and it was completed in 1283. The man-made waterway stretched 125 kilometres from Jining to the town of Da'anshan, both in the province of Shandong.

To the south the Jizhou Canal joined up with the Zhongyun Canal via the natural course of the Sishui River, while in the north it joined the Nanyun Canal through the Huitong Canal, opened soon afterwards. Before the digging of the Jizhou and Huitong canals, foodgrains were shipped to the imperial capital along the Y-shaped canal built during the Sui dynasty along the course of the Yellow River in northern Jiangsu, leading to north China through Henan and the Nanyun Canal. The roundabout route was more than 700 kilometres longer.

As Shandong province at the time lacked water sources, the Jizhou Canal took its water from Weishan Lake and the Sishui River in the south and from Dongping Lake and the Daqing River in the north. In the Ming dynasty a project was built to divert water from the Wenshui River to regulate the water of the Grand Canal.

The Huitong Canal was dug six years after the completion of the Jizhou Canal. During those six years two methods were used to transport foodgrains to the imperial capital. One was overland from the site of the Huitong Canal excavations to Linqing, then by the Nanyun Canal. The other was a sea route via Dongping Lake and the course of the Daqing River. The land route was low-lying and muddy in late summer and early autumn, and so traffic on it was very difficult. And foodgrains transported by the sea route always suffered heavy losses from storms. These problems strengthened Kublai Khan's resolve to open the Huitong Canal.

The opening of the Jizhou Canal helped cut the grain transport route by almost one-third, saving considerable time and expense. It ushered in a new epoch of water transport of imperial foodgrains from the south to the north on the I-shaped Grand Canal.

The silted-up old channel of the Jizhou Canal near the Yellow River.

(Top right) A bumper rice harvest on Yutai Canal Farm, built by the descendants of boatmen and fishermen on the abandoned canal bed.

(Right) The old ship lock that takes the Jizhou Canal to the Yellow River via the Liangshan Mountains. The lock has become obsolete because of the increasing amount of silt on the riverbed.

(Left) Archaeologists study the ruins of the ancient state of Xue in the Spring and Autumn Period (770-47 B.C.). There are many such historical relics along the banks of the Jizhou Canal in Shandong province.

(*Left*) **Mount Tai rises above the clouds.**

(*Right*) **Boat dwellers on the Jizhou Canal.**

(*Extreme right*) **Net-making is one of the jobs of the fishermen's wives.**

(*Bottom right*) **The Confucius Temple at Qufu, home town of the famed philosopher.**

(*Below*) **A train steams west on the newly-built Jining-Heze Railway across the Grand Canal.**

Weishan Lake

After entering Shandong province the Grand Canal passes through Weishan Lake. The lake, stretching 120 kilometres from north to south and about twenty kilometres across at its widest part, covers an area of 1,266 square kilometres and has a capacity of 36 billion cubic metres of water during the high water season. In times of flood the lake can accommodate excess water from Shandong and neighbouring Jiangsu, Henan and Anhui provinces.

The lake was formed in 1194 when the flooding Yellow River changed course by pouring into the channels of the Huai River and the Sihe River before emptying into the sea. Later the heavy silt of the Yellow River filled the Sihe River estuary, cutting off its outlet to the sea.

The lake abounds with carp, mandarin fish and other fishes as well as turtles, shrimps and crabs. More than one hundred water plants including lotus, water chestnuts, reeds and Gorgon fruit thrive in the lake. Among them are more than seventy medicinal herbs.

The lake was always a frequent source of flooding because it lacked an outlet to the sea, but recent water conservation projects have resulted in the building of four embankments and the digging of an outlet. The sluice gates built at Hanzhuang in 1980 are capable of releasing 9,000 to 10,000 cubic metres of water per second, thus ensuring safety for the lake area, Shandong and Jiangsu provinces in general, and navigation along this section of the canal.

Hanzhuang Sluice, at the southern end of Weishan Lake, rebuilt in 1982, controls flooding from the provinces of Shandong, Henan and Jiangsu, and ensures the safety of millions along the banks of the canal.

(Top right) **Geese, once confined to south China, spread northwards with the digging of the Grand Canal.**

(Right) **Happy fisherwomen with practical sunshades.**

(Left) **A snack stall in the northern part of the Huitong Canal.**

(Following page) **The course of the Grand Canal in the Yuan, Ming and Qing dynasties ran through Weishan Lake before joining the Zhongyun Canal.**

Liangshan Marsh

In its southward advance the Grand Canal crosses the Yellow River in Shandong province. To the west of the canal after the crossing is a historical place known to almost every Chinese as the centre of activities of the "Outlaws of the Marsh", a band of Robin Hood-type heroes who valiantly challenged the Song dynasty rulers during the 11th century.

This is the Liangshan Marsh, stretching about 400 kilometres from north to south and from east to west as a result of the frequent overflows of the Yellow, Jihe and Daqing rivers. During the reign of Zhihe (1054-1056) under the Song Emperor Renzong, 108 heroic outlaws led thousands of local fishermen and peasants in rebellion against the Song rulers. Time and again they defeated the efforts of the Song army to capture them. The rebels elected Song Jiang as their leader, and hoisted a banner in-

scribed with the slogan "Take from the Rich to Give to the Poor; Uphold Truth on Behalf of Heaven!" The heroes were vividly immortalised in the classic novel *The Outlaws of the Marsh*, resulting in the site of their headquarters becoming a source of curiosity for hundreds of years.

There are some mountains in the marsh; the main peak is called Hutouyan, or the Crag of Tigerhead. The ruins of some of the foundations of the walls of Song Jiang's encampment are still to be found. The only pass leading to the main peak is called Heifengkou, or Blackwind Pass. All the paths from the other peaks lead to this pass. Ruins of ancient buildings still stand on most of the peaks.

The Liangshan Marsh, called Liaoerwa in *The Outlaws of the Marsh*, was heavily silted up and became a plain when the Yellow River changed its course. Today only a corner of the former Liaoerwa still exists — Dongping Lake, 20 kilometres northeast of the Liangshan Mountains.

Dongping Lake, all that is left of the old Liangshan Marsh which, when the rebel peasants used it as a hideout in the Song dynasty, covered an area 400 kilometres square.

(Top right) A mountain path used by the outlaws' cavalry.

(Right) The Crag of Tigerhead, where the Song dynasty rebels set up their strongholds.

(Left) Liangshan county town, built on the former marshland.

The provincial tourist authorities have done much restoration work in Liangshan district in recent years, and a statue of Li Kui, one of the Liangshan heroes, has been erected at Blackwind Pass. Work is under way to restore the old drill ground, the watch-tower and cash distribution pavilion, and scenic spots such as "The Lotus Terrace" and "Sunset on the Green Dragon Hill". A stone tablet inscribed with the words "The Liangshan Marsh" by the noted calligrapher Shu Tong has been erected at the foot of the mountain. A newly paved stone road connects with the path the outlaws rode along. There are plans to restore the "Hall of Righteous Gathering" and the back barracks, two major buildings in the days of the marsh heroes.

Tourists may now hire sightseeing boats to thread through the lotuses on Dongping Lake to visit the former sites where the Liangshan heroes drilled their naval units. They can also enjoy a delicious meal of fresh seafood at a lakeside restaurant.

Liangshan Harbour, previously a port on the canal.

(Top right) Low-lying areas are overgrown with reeds, bringing to mind a line from *The Water Margin:* "A little boat flows amid reed flowers."

(Right) The statue of Li Kui, one of the legendary Outlaws of the Marsh, at Blackwind Pass.

(Left) Flooding from the Yellow River in 1982 once again inundated a large area at the foot of the Liangshan Mountains. Here fishermen spread their nets in the new lake.

(Left) The Suqian canal harbour. At 200 metres, this is the widest section of the Zhongyun Canal.

(Right) An old channel of the Yellow River. From the 12th to the 19th century the Yellow River emptied into the sea in northern Jiangsu province through the Zhongyun Canal.

(Bottom right) The canal's flood-warning bell, cast in 1202 of an alloy of copper and iron, is 1.8 metres long and weighs 2.5 tons.

(Below) Qingjiangshi, the busiest harbour on the Zhongyun Canal during the Ming and Qing dynasties.

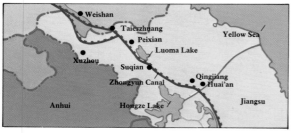

Zhongyun Canal

The Grand Canal is divided into two sections in the northern part of Jiangsu province — the Zhongyun Canal to the north and the Liyun Canal to the south.

The Zhongyun Canal stretches 223 kilometres from Taierzhuang in Shandong province to Huai'an county in Jiangsu province. About two hundred metres wide and from three to six metres deep, it is a busy waterway.

It flows south from Taierzhuang to the Luoma Lake through Yunhe town in Peixian county. The Luoma Lake has a surface area of 275 square kilometres and stores 7,000 million cubic metres of water. It teems with aquatic products.

Zhongyun Canal then passes through the city of Suqian, which means a place "moved from elsewhere overnight". It is said that in

the Han dynasty (2nd century), when the Yellow River was in flood, some 90,000 people fled one night to seek higher ground. They settled in this spot and named it "Suqian". A city wall was built around it during the reign of Emperor Yongle (15th century).

Most places along the canal from Suqian to Huaiyin, where the Qingjiang Big Lock is located, have a name signifying "water" in Chinese characters. The low-lying areas of the provinces of Henan, Shandong and Anhui suffered from flooding for centuries. "Water" in the character components of the names reminds people of the necessity to take constant precautions against flood. Today, the areas present a new, more beautiful sight. A network of rivers, brooks and streams criss-crosses the rice fields, and boats ply back and forth on them. The volume of freight on the waterways there accounts for 75 percent of the total on the entire Zhongyun Canal.

The canal continues south to Siyang county, where the famous Yanghe liquor is produced by the 300-year-old Yanghe Winery. Made with water from the "Spring of Beauty" nearby, the Yanghe liquor enjoys a fine reputation both at home and abroad. It was awarded a gold medal at the 1915 Panama Fair.

After passing through Siyang, the canal reaches the Qingjiang Big Lock. This well-known lock in the city of Huaiyin was built under the supervision of Song Li, Minister of Communications in the reign of Emperor Yongle of the Ming dynasty. It was laid with stone slabs, each weighing 150 kilograms, and lime and sand mixed with glutinous rice water. The "Big" in its name is a reference to its length — 200 metres on both sides. No ordinary lock, it has no gate, only a mouth used to regulate water commensurate with the flow capacity of the canal. This allows it to remain navigable around the clock, and is an illustration of the high level of hydraulic engineering technology attained in 15th century China.

In the early 20th century a new channel was dug, bigger and faster engine-powered ships came into use and 400-metre-long fleets emerged. The government built the Huaiyin and the Huai'an ship locks along the new channel to meet the expanding needs of water transport. Although the Qingjiang Big Lock, used for about 500 years, has been replaced by the two new locks, many veteran boatmen still prefer to sail along its familiar route, and many visitors travel through it to view the historical sites along the old Grand Canal.

Next to Huaiyin along the Zhongyun Canal is Huai'an. These two ancient cities have developed rapidly into new industrial centres since the advent of flood control and the resumption of water transport in north Jiangsu.

The Huai'an Ship Lock, one of the biggest on the Zhongyun Canal.

(*Left*) The famous Qingjiang Sluice, built in 1402, has no locks and is open to navigation at all times.

(Top right) **Yunhe, the first large port on the Zhongyun Canal, is a busy junction where the waterway connects with the Long-Hai Railway.**

(Right) **Fishermen on the Zhongyun Canal, who enter the water fully dressed, are very skilled in catching fish and crabs with their hands.**

(Left) The major sluice gate on the Trunk Canal crossing the Zhongyun Canal in northern Jiangsu province was built in the 1950s to regulate the water level, drain floodwaters and irrigate the surrounding farmlands.

(Right) Farmers in Huai'an line up to sell grain to the state.

(Bottom right) Daiwang Temple, on the banks of the Zhongyun Canal, was said to have been a palace that was built for Emperor Qianlong of the Qing dynasty.

(Bottom left) Suqian, by the side of the Zhongyun Canal, was the birthplace of the ancient warrior Xiang Yu.

(Below) The Zaohe Sluice, built in the 17th century when the Grand Canal ran through Luoma Lake, is now a historical site.

Hongze Lake

Hongze Lake — the biggest natural reservoir of the Grand Canal — is located near the southern end of the Zhongyun Canal. It plays an important part in regulating the water flow of the Zhongyun and Liyun canals. Hongze is a "lake in the air", a type rarely seen in the world: its bed is six to eight metres above the level of the nearby towns and villages. The lake is held in check by a solid dyke, 200 kilometres long, and has a normal water storage capacity of 32,850 million cubic metres and a maximum capacity of 78,350 million.

Lake Hongze once consisted of many scattered small lakes. In 1194, when the Yellow River "annexed" the Huaihe River on its new course to the sea, stopping the seaward flow of the upper Huaihe, the obstructed water merged the small lakes into a single big one, the Hongze.

The present embankment is the result of constant rebuilding and repairing over the centuries in the intervals between almost 100 breaches. In the 661 years from 1194 to 1855, silt from the Yellow River elevated the lake bed by several centimetres every year, resulting in today's "lake in the air", and every breach of the embankment was catastrophic. A bursting of the banks in 1680 (the 19th year of the reign of Emperor

Fishing boats on the canal.

(*Top right*) **Fishermen go out at daybreak on the lake.**

(*Right*) **Hunting wild ducks on the lake.**

(*Left*) **The ruins of an ancient subsidiary embankment. The lake often burst its banks during the Ming and Qing dynasties, the flood in 1851 submerging the city of Sizhou.**

Kangxi of the Qing dynasty) resulted in the instant inundation of the city of Sizhou. Now, during dry seasons when the water level in the lake is low, relics of the ancient city are occasionally hauled out of the water. After 1855, when the Yellow River changed its course again to flow to the sea through Shandong province, Hongze Lake became stabilised, with no further elevation of its bed and no more bursting of the dykes.

Since the establishment of the People's Republic in 1949, the government has launched a series of projects to bring the lake under control: the building of an intake works and a flood discharge sluice gate in 1952-53; another sluice gate and a general irrigation canal for vast areas in northern Jiangsu province in 1958; a systematic reinforcement of the embankment by sloping it and covering it with large stones and the cultivation of an anti-wave forest belt fifty metres wide and fourteen-and-a-half metres tall from 1962 to 1966 and from 1976 to 1981; and the addition of anti-earthquake works during the late 1970s.

Lake Hongze has now become a treasured resource of the people of northern Jiangsu. Not only does it guarantee navigation on the Grand Canal, but it has become a key water control project playing a comprehensive role in irrigation, aquatic breeding and power generation.

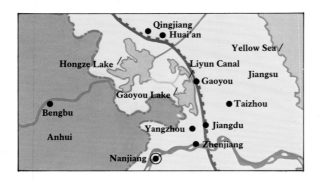

Liyun Canal

The people of ancient China liked to compare the Grand Canal to a rein which controlled the nation's five big rivers — the Haihe, Yellow, Huaihe, Yangtze and Qiantang. The Liyun Canal, literally the "Inner Canal", is the oldest section of this halter. It is because of this section that the Grand Canal can boast a history of 2,400 years.

In 486 B.C., King Fuchai of the state of Wu during the Spring and Autumn period dug the first man-made waterway, called the Hangou Ditch, to connect the Yangtze and Huaihe rivers to transport his troops to the central plains to contend for supremacy over the middle reaches of the Yellow River.

Hangou was the predecessor of the Liyun Canal, extending 185 kilometres from Jiangdu (now Yangzhou) in the south to Huai'an in the north. In the 7th century, Emperor Yangdi of the Sui dynasty mobilised 100,000 labourers to straighten Hangou into a 150-kilometre waterway and build roads and plant willow trees along its embankments. As a special mark of honour to the willows he renamed the tree (originally called *liu* in Chinese) *yang'liu* after his own surname. From then on it has been a long-standing tradition to plant willows all along the embankments of the Liyun Canal.

A bird's-eye view of the Liyun Canal shows that it connects a string of pearl-like natural lakes. It was said that about 6,000 years ago, a seismic wave from the sea flooded this part of the lower reaches of the Yangtze River. When the flood receded, lakes were formed by the subsidence of the earth's crust. King Fuchai had the lakes north of the Yangtze connected with the canal. The lakes were used as a natural reservoir for the waterway, and the Liyun Canal became known as the "string of lakes".

The embankments of the Liyun Canal, about eight metres high, look like high walls from the ground. Driving along the raised highways built on them from Huai'an to Yangzhou, visitors sometimes have the feeling that they are flying over the farmlands below. The surface of the Liyun Canal is five metres above ground level, while its embankments are three metres above the water surface. So it is also known as a "river above the ground".

Situated in the lower reaches of the Huaihe River, the Liyun Canal runs across a plain which is higher on its west bank than on its east. During the Sui dynasty, water from the Yellow River was diverted to the canal through the Huaihe River to facilitate navigation. But the silt from the Yellow River raised the Huaihe riverbed, which caused frequent flooding. When the roaring water ran down from the west, vast expanses of farmland lying below the eastern bank of the canal were submerged. In 1931, when the eastern embankment was breached in twenty-six places near Gaoyou county, more than 70,000 lives were lost, over 700,000 people were made homeless and no crops could be grown on the farmland for three years.

Flood prevention projects such as dykes and sluice gates have been added almost every year along the Liyun Canal. The biggest stone dyke was built in the Ming dynasty. Ruins of a section of the stone dyke built in 1577, the fourth year of the reign of Emperor Wanli, were discovered in 1982 when the canal bed was being dredged. The 1,900-metre section of the dyke was built on both sides with stone slabs, each two metres long and 0.4 metres wide, with large paving bricks between two layers of stone embankments four metres high. The bricks were cemented together by lime mixed with glutinous rice water. Even a solidly constructed dyke like this, however, still could not resist the floods, and gradually, over many years, it sank deep into the silt on the canal bed.

Among the most conspicuous ancient flood warning devices along the Liyun Canal was an iron ox cast in the Ming dynasty. Originally there were nine such iron oxen. They were used for measuring the water level along the canal. When the water surface reached the nose of the ox, a flood was in the offing. In the old days local villagers worshipped the iron ox as a god, and burned incense and kowtowed before it to pray that the water would never reach its nose.

The spot where the Liyun Canal empties into the Yangtze River has changed location several times because the silt often raised parts of the northern bank of the Yangtze. In the late Tang dynasty the outlet shifted from Yangzhou, a prosperous river port, to Guazhou, and the latter took over the former's prosperous ferry business. However, a serious landslip on the northern bank of the Yangtze in 1884, the tenth year of the reign of Emperor Guangxu of the Qing dynasty, sent the Guazhou ferry together with the whole town into the Yangtze. Now the Liyun Canal empties into the Yangtze at Liuwei. This place is better situated, and was selected in 1958 when the new channel was dredged.

Despite its frequent flooding, the Liyun Canal has been a very important link in the history of water transport on the Grand Canal. During the Northern Song dynasty (960-1127), more than 480,000 tons of grain were shipped to the imperial capital through the Liyun Canal every year. Salt from twenty-three salt works south of the Huaihe River was transported via this section of the canal to cater to the needs of people in over 200 counties in six provinces during the Ming dynasty.

Salt merchants north and south of the Huaihe River were the wealthiest people in the Qing dynasty. When a project to dredge the Liyun Canal was begun in 1739, the third year of the reign of Emperor Qianlong, Huang Rende, a local salt merchant, contributed 300,000 taels (about 9,600 kilograms) of silver to the fund.

Although there is now rail transport on the Yangtze-Huaihe plains, the Liyun Canal continues to be an important waterway. A

(Left) **The Liyun Canal embankment covered with dense thickets of willow trees, a tradition that has continued since the 7th century.**

(Top right) **The Huai'an-Yangzhou highway runs along the east bank of the Liyun Canal.**

(Right) **The widening of the Liyun Canal in 1958 brought this Tang pagoda, which once stood in the county town of Gaoyou, up to the water's edge.**

(Following page) **The Liyun Canal is navigable in all seasons.**

A granite embankment on the Liyun Canal.

(Top right) Reconstruction work being carried out in 1982.

(Right) Transplanting rice on the banks of the Liyun Canal.

(Left) The Ming dynasty iron ox, one of nine once used to measure the water level of the Liyun Canal.

key water control project was built in the 1970s in Yangzhou, where Emperor Yangdi of the Sui dynasty had his holiday palaces. The project was intended to divert excess water from south China to north China, and consisted of four pumping stations with a total capacity of 49,800 kilowatts and a designated flow rate of 473 cubic metres of water per second. It is now irrigating 46,700 hectares of farmland and regulating the periods of flood and drought along the Liyun Canal. By using the pumping stations, it is planned to divert 100 cubic metres of water per second from the Yangtze to Beijing and Tianjin in north China by 1985.

A project to widen the channel of the Liyun Canal began in 1958. More than 240,000 labourers worked to dredge the canal in 1982. The new 150-kilometre waterway will be 220 metres wide with a depth of four to six metres and a seventy-metre-wide riverbed. It will be the first section of the Grand Canal to be able to handle ships in the 1,000-ton class.

(Top left) The ruins of a Ming dynasty stone embankment. On either side of the embankment are wooden stakes which were used in the foundations.

(Right) Children graze their water buffaloes along the canal banks, where water is plentiful and the grass is lush.

(Left) A happy domestic scene afloat.

The Liyun Canal's 825-metre long Shiqiao Lock has a passageway 250 metres long by twenty metres wide. Ships in the 3,000-ton class can pass through it.

(Left) Busy wharves along the Liyun Canal.

(Right) **The remains of one of the 12th century boats used to transport grain to the imperial capitals.**

(Below) **Mokou, in Huai'an, was the terminal of the Hangou Ditch.**

(Left) Steps of an ancient ferry pier in Guazhou, Jiangsu province.

(Right) Double-yolk duck eggs are a speciality of Gaoyou county, where eggs with even three or four yolks are not rare.

(Below) The new Guazhou town, built two kilometres from old Guazhou, which was washed away by the Yangtze in 1884.

79

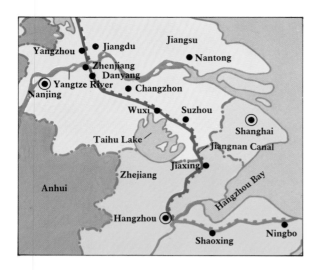

Jiangnan Canal

Crossing the Yangtze River at Liuwei near Yangzhou, the Grand Canal runs on till it reaches the Jianbi Ship Lock, east of the city of Zhenjiang, where it enters the last stage of its journey — the Jiangnan (South of the Yangtze River) Canal. This section of the canal flows through Danyang, Changzhou, Wuxi, Suzhou and Jiaxing, winds past the east bank of Lake Tai and ends at Hangzhou, making a total length of 340 kilometres. Filled with water and crowded with boats all year round, the Jiangnan Canal is the busiest and most spectacular section of the Grand Canal.

Along its entire length down the lower reaches of the Yangtze River, there has been since ancient times a network of rivers and streams densely dotted with dykes and islets. Suzhou and Hangzhou, beauty spots the ancients praised as "living paradises on earth", are nestled by its side, while Lake Tai, one of China's four big freshwater lakes, spreads out as its natural reservoir. The lake finds its water sources in the numerous springs on the Tianmu Mountain near Hangzhou. Therefore its clear water carries very little silt into the Jiangnan Canal, which, benefiting from this gift of nature, enjoys an abundant water supply and a highly navigable channel.

As far back as 506 B.C. when Helu, the father of King Fuchai of the state of Wu, was in power, the natural river course between the Yangtze and Lake Tai was dredged and used to send grain as well as soldiers north in support of his expedition. Later, during Fuchai's time, transportation between Gusu, capital of the state of Wu (present-day Suzhou) and the city of Han-cheng (present-day Yangzhou) became very dependent on this water route as a result of

(Right) **The Jiangnan Canal at one stage runs parallel with the Beijing-Hangzhou railway line.**

(Bottom right) **The ancient outlet of the Nanyun Canal to the Yangtze River.**

(Below) **Springtime on the banks of the Jiangnan Canal.**

the opening up of the Hangou Ditch on the northern bank of the Yangtze.

In 210 B.C. Emperor Qinshihuang connected Fuchai's water route to a new 62-kilometre-long canal to strengthen his control of the area south of the Yangtze. The canal was dug by 3,000 convicts, and because they were all dressed in red it was dubbed "The River of Red Convicts". It was out of this extended waterway that the present-day Jiangnan Canal grew.

In A.D. 494, when the emperor of Liang, one of the Southern dynasties, was building his tomb in Danyang, the River of Red Convicts was used to transport huge blocks of stone, each weighing several tons, to the tomb site to be carved into the shapes of various animals. These stone animals, standing guard at the entrance to the tomb, provide a vivid reflection of the civilisation of the Southern dynasties. They were carved more than a century before the world-famous Six Stone Steeds of the Zhao Tomb, the tomb of Emperor Li Shimin of the Tang dynasty in Sian.

In A.D. 610 Emperor Yangdi of the Sui dynasty employed 100,000 labourers to deepen and widen this waterway, and had it extended from the banks of Lake Tai to Hangzhou in Zhejiang province, linking up the canal with the Qiantang River. He gave it a new name — the Jiangnan Canal. It was later connected with the canal from northern China during the Yuan dynasty to form the Grand Canal, and it has been in active use from then until this very day.

The two extremities of the Jiangnan Canal, which lies flat on the plains around Lake Tai, are in hilly areas, which means its channel is elevated at both ends. The section between Zhenjiang and Danyang, for example, was dug on a loess ridge twenty metres high with the banks ten metres above the water level. For many centuries it had relied on tidal water from the Yangtze to make up for the consequent shortage of water. For this reason, each time Emperor Qianlong of the Qing dynasty visited the area south of the Yangtze he had to issue a decree before he reached this section of the Jiangnan Canal, permitting officials of Zhejiang province not to wait on him at Danyang, where the canal was narrow and shallow, but welcome him rather at the prefecture of Suzhou, where the canal was much wider.

Due to the fact that Suzhou is situated at that part of the canal where the land is flat, Suzhou prefecture was renamed Pingjiang ("Flat River") prefecture during the Song dynasty. However, north or south of Suzhou the terrain rose gradually, so much so that boatmen in the old days had to get out on the banks and tow the boats upstream when they reached the stone bridge at Wujiang River, where navigation became as difficult as climbing a slope.

Several dozen kilometres of stone embankments were built along the river during the middle of the 11th century to serve as a towpath for the boatmen. Many bridges were built on the way, the most well known being the Baodai (Treasured Belt) Bridge which, constructed between A.D. 816 and 819, is the biggest bridge along the entire Grand Canal as well as the longest of the existing ancient bridges of China. It is 317 metres long and 4.1 metres wide, with a total of fifty-three spans. It was said that to raise funds to build this bridge, Wang Zhongshu, the prefectural governor of Suzhou during the Tang dynasty, contributed a treasured belt that had been handed down from his ancestors and was worth several cities.

(Right) **The busy docks in Wuxi, Jiangsu province.**

(Bottom right) **The Jiangnan Canal passes through a small town.**

(Below) **Jianbi Lock Gate in Zhenjiang, the Jiangnan Canal's outlet to the Yangtze River.**

Affected by river and sea tides, the sections of the Jiangnan Canal where it meets the Yangtze and Qiantang rivers were often silted up. The confluence was thus moved westward five times, from Zhenjiang to Jianbi, then to Dantu, Ganlukou, Lesser Jingkou and Greater Jingkou respectively. Sluice gates were built at every confluence to control the river tides as well as to increase the amount of water flowing through the canal.

The section at Danyang was frequently affected by the silt, which made navigation so difficult that hundreds of boats were often seen crowded together waiting for passage. When the noted national hero of the Qing dynasty, Lin Zexu, was governor of Jiangsu province, he once assumed personal command at the Jingkou Dam to supervise and direct the orderly passage of the boats.

The confluence between the canal and the Qiantang River had such a serious silting problem that it finally became unnavigable during the Ming dynasty. Since the 15th century the Grand Canal has linked only the Hai, Huang, Huai and Yangtze rivers. A project to reopen the link with the Qiantang River started in 1983.

A peaceful scene on the Jiangnan Canal.

(Top right) **A family of boat dwellers on their "front porch".**

(Right) **This stone bridge in Jiangsu's Wujiang county was used as a towpath to pull the grain boats in the old days.**

(Left) **A canalside marketplace.**

Generally speaking, the Jiangnan Canal is easily navigable, and it has helped agricultural production in the area south of the lower reaches of the Yangtze to become much more advanced than that of the area along the Yellow River in north China.

It was estimated in the Tang dynasty that nine-tenths of the taxes levied throughout the country came from this area. Taxes in the form of grain shipped to the imperial court through the Jiangnan Canal totalled approximately 240,000 tons yearly during the Ming and Qing dynasties. A ballad of the time sung by people along the canal had it that "lengthy is the canal, boats crowded like hell, imperial grain to carry, enough to fill the granary", a sign of the prosperity of the land along the canal and the heavy traffic that it carried.

In his efforts to carry out large-scale water conservation works, the king of the state of Wuyue, Qian Miao (A.D. 907-960) sent a special detachment of troops along Lake Tai to widen the Jiangnan Canal and harness a series of tributaries of the canal and other

rivers. This was the first step leading to the construction of waterways in the area. The area around Suzhou and Hangzhou has consequently become one of the most prosperous parts of China.

It was from this period that the popular saying "High above there is heaven, while down below there are Suzhou and Hangzhou" began to be used. Its first appearance on record, however, was during the Song dynasty, when the annals of Wu prefecture used the expression "Heaven in the sky, Suzhou and Hangzhou on earth". With the rapid development of industry and commerce, merchants from far and near were drawn to the towns and cities along the canal.

During the Qing dynasty, the Jiangnan Canal developed further as a main waterway of the Grand Canal. The Qing court was so dependent on the canal financially that when the British naval fleet sailed right into the port of Zhenjiang, blocking the outlet of the canal where it empties into the Yangtze River and looting more than a thousand

An ancient stone towpath on the banks of the Jiangnan Canal.

(Top right) This old bridge was rebuilt in 1971.

(Right) A woodcut showing one of the ancient grain boats making its way along the Jiangnan Canal — its final destination Beijing.

grain-loaded boats, the court was deprived of its tax income and forced to sign the Nanjing Treaty.

Though the Nanjing-Shanghai Railway running parallel to the Jiangnan Canal has been operating since the early 20th century, the canal still plays a pivotal role in linking the Yangtze River with inland waterways in the southern part of Zhejiang and Jiangsu provinces. Even to this day the canal carries a heavy traffic in boats taking grain and other commodities of the area north, and bringing back coal.

With so many scenic spots along its banks, the Jiangnan Canal has become the first section of the Grand Canal to be opened to foreign tourists. The pleasure of making what has been described as "a trip of mystery and wonder" along its route has attracted tens of thousands of visitors from abroad.

漕舫圖

(Left) **These stone animals in Lingkou, Danyang county, have been standing guard over an imperial tomb for almost 1,500 years. The nearest one, a Chinese unicorn, is 2.42 metres tall and 2.9 metres long.**

(Right) **The Jiangnan Canal is criss-crossed by many rivers and streams.**

(Below) **Billowing sails on a windy day.**

(Following page) **Spring brings a green blanket to the paddy fields bordering the canal.**

(Top left) **Farmers sell bags made of rice straw, a traditional sideline product of the region.**

(Top right) **Barges tie up on the Jiangnan Canal in the southwest of Suzhou.**

(Right) **An ancient cobblestoned street in a canalside town.**

(Left) **This ferry pavilion was built in imitation of 18th century Qing dynasty architecture.**

(Left) **A wheat threshing ground on the canal banks.**

(Right) **A dredger at work clearing silt from the canal.**

(Below) **The Treasure Belt Bridge in Suzhou, the longest of the Grand Canal's ancient bridges. Nearby is a new highway bridge completed in 1977.**

(Bottom left) **A forest of masts on Lake Taihu, the Jiangnan Canal's natural reservoir.**

(Extreme left) A bamboo forest on Mogan Mountain near the southern end of the canal in Zhejiang province.

(Left) An entertainer sings for boat passengers. Waterborne entertainment has a history of more than a thousand years. Emperors Yangdi, Zhengde and Qianlong were all accompanied by singers on their voyages south along the canal.

(Right) A flotilla of fishing boats.

(Below) Desheng Dam in Hangzhou, where the Grand Canal ends.

(Bottom left) The Grand Canal bisects the ancient city of Huzhou, Zhejiang province.

The Cities of the Grand Canal

Beijing—Starting Point of the Canal

The capital city of Beijing, political, economic and cultural centre of the People's Republic of China, is one of the six fabled ancient capitals of the country. Situated north of the north China plains 150 kilometres from Bohai Bay, it currently has a population of 9.23 million.

The Grand Canal starts in Tongxian county, twenty kilometres east of the city proper, and meanders southwards. As one of the world's great engineering feats, it is as much a symbol of the ancient civilisation of China as the Great Wall that snakes its way north of the city.

Men lived in Beijing 18,000 years ago, as proved by the discovery of Peking (Beijing) man by paleoanthropologists. The ancient city of Ji, capital of the state of Yan during the Spring and Autumn period, first appeared on this spot ten centuries before Christ. In the seventh century, when Emperor Yangdi of the Sui dynasty opened the Y-shaped Grand Canal, Beijing, as the northern terminal of the canal, began to play its role in the story of this great waterway.

Beijing served as the starting point of the Grand Canal in 1271 when Kublai Khan, the first emperor of the Yuan dynasty, set up his capital in what was then called Dadu (Great Capital). He dredged and reopened the entire course of the Grand Canal so that he could transport grain and articles of tribute to his court from south China. This opened up a chapter of prosperity in the annals of Beijing. As the succeeding Ming and Qing dynasties continued to make Beijing their capital, the foundations were laid for its present scale and grandeur.

During the Yuan dynasty, Beijing was the world's biggest city. The famous traveller Marco Polo, an Italian merchant from 13th century Venice, wrote the following description of Beijing: "Shops and stalls stand on the two sides of the streets... There are big tourist inns in the suburbs as far as 1.6 kilometres from the city... All kinds of valuable goods are sent here from other provinces of the empire... There are many more commodities on sale in the market than anywhere else... Registration shows that no less than 1,000 cartloads of raw silk

Sudichunxiao (Spring Dawn on the Su Causeway) is one of the ten well-known scenic spots on the West Lake. In the 11th century, when Su Shi, one of the Song dynasty's illustrious men of letters, was appointed magistrate of Hangzhou, he dredged the West Lake and used the earth to build a 2.8-kilometre-long dyke, which was thereafter known as the Su Causeway.

99

High-rise buildings on the Beijing skyline.

are brought to the capital by horses and other pack animals."

In the early 14th century the Tonghui Canal, the northernmost section of the Grand Canal, was dug from the northwestern part of the city to the east. It brought water and prosperity to arid Beijing. A network of waterways with a total of 156 bridges criss-crossed a vast area within and around the city. Boats loaded with grain and articles of tribute sailed to and fro under the bridges which connected the city streets. Boats filled the channel and grain piled high on the banks at the canal's wharf of Jishuitan (now Shishahai) in the central part of the city. Freighters could reach the wharf directly from southern China through the canal. Shops and inns did good business there. The area where the Bell Tower and Drum Tower now stand was the earliest commercial centre of Beijing in the Yuan dynasty.

Beijing grew into China's biggest consumer city and commercial centre in the Ming and Qing dynasties. Some 10,000 official boats manned by 120,000 soldiers transported grain and other goods to the capital all year round in the Ming dynasty. *Nanmu* timber, bricks and tiles and other building materials were all sent to Beijing from the southern provinces by way of the Grand Canal to construct palaces and mausoleums for the Ming emperors.

In the mid-14th century the Tonghui Canal silted up and the starting point of the Grand Canal was shifted to Tongxian

(Top right) **Part of Beijing's modern highway system.**

(Right) **The gardens along the capital's Changan Avenue.**

county (called Tongzhou at that time), east of the city proper. Grain carriers and cargo ships moored in Tongxian, and the goods were discharged and transported to Beijing overland. Commercial streets several kilometres in length were developed between Tongxian and the city centre. Inns and restaurants along the streets served the merchants and boatmen. A tax office was set up there to collect commercial taxes for goods going to the capital. The commercial centre of Beijing moved from the vicinity of the Bell Tower and Drum Tower to Chaoyangmen, east of the city. Many granaries were erected east of the city, and government offices were established to administer grain storage. During the reign of Emperor Qianlong in the mid-18th century heyday of the Qing dynasty, Beijing had thirteen official warehouses and 932 granaries, storing 300,000 tons of grain a year.

The Ming emperors shipped enormous quantities of silk, tea, sugar, bamboo, timber and ceramics from southern China to Beijing. Temple trade fairs were held regularly, and traditional festivals such as the Lantern Festival, on the first full moon of the lunar calendar, the Qingming Festival in memory of ancestors and the Mid-Autumn Moon Festival became occasions for holding big trade fairs.

In the Ming dynasty even the emperors and their eunuchs engaged in commercial business. Six imperial shops on the eastern side of the Forbidden City dealt in various commodities from south and north China. A typical annual turnover of these shops would be 10,000 marten pelts, 60,000 fox furs, 800,000 bolts of cloth, 6,000 bales of cotton, 2,380 tons of glutinous rice, 2,000 cartloads of salted meat, 10,000 boxes of tea, 500,000 hogs, 300,000 sheep as well as large quantities of pearls and medicinal herbs.

In the late 19th century, when the water transport of grain and articles of tribute to the imperial court stopped and the north-south railway opened, the day of the sailing boats from south China ended. But the many historical sites and relics in Beijing are today a reminder of how the Grand Canal brought prosperity to this ancient capital.

The magnificent buildings of the imperial palaces of the Yuan, Ming and Qing dynasties in the centre of Beijing bear witness to the role the Grand Canal played in water transport. The architectural complex of pal-

(Top left) The Beijing-Miyun Canal, the capital's water lifeline. It runs through the old course of the upper Tonghui River, the northernmost section of the Grand Canal in the Yuan dynasty.

(Right) A portrait of Kublai Khan, founder of the Yuan dynasty, who ordered the excavation of a direct waterway between Beijing and Hangzhou. He also founded the city of Dadu, present-day Beijing.

(Left) Inside the famous Liubiju sauce and pickle shop near Qianmen Gate, which dates back to the 19th century.

aces known as the Forbidden City was first formed in 1406 (the fourth year of the reign of Ming Emperor Yongle), and then rebuilt and expanded by the Qing emperors. The existing palace buildings cover a total floor space of 150,000 square metres and have 9,000 rooms. They are the world's biggest complex of wooden buildings, and a treasure trove of ancient architecture.

In the centre of New China's national emblem is a design portraying the Tiananmen Gate — symbol of China's ancient civilisation and rebirth. The gate was formerly called Chengtianmen, the southern gate of the Forbidden City. It was on the tower of this gate that Mao Zedong, the great leader of the Chinese people, raised the first five-star red flag on October 1, 1949 to proclaim to the world that the Chinese people had risen to their feet.

The spacious Tiananmen Square connected with the Forbidden City was formerly a T-shaped square where the imperial court held important ceremonies. The Chinese government of today uses it for ceremonies to welcome distinguished guests from foreign countries. At the centre of the square stands the Monument to the People's Heroes, and to its west is the Great Hall of the People where deputies of all the regions of China discuss important state affairs. The Museum of Chinese History is on the eastern side of the square, while in the south is the Memorial Hall of Chairman Mao Zedong. In front of the Jinshui (Golden Water) Bridge of the Tiananmen Gate is a five-kilometre thoroughfare, Changan Avenue, lined with trees and houses of golden tiles and red walls.

Fifty kilometres from the city proper are the Ming Tombs, where thirteen Ming dynasty emperors lie buried deep underground. Changling, the biggest one, is the mausoleum of Emperor Yongle, who initiated the building of the Forbidden City. The Lingen Hall in this mausoleum is China's largest building made of *nanmu* timber, with thirty-two pillars, each more than four-

(Right) **A typical courtyard house in Beijing.**

(Bottom right) **Breeding pet birds is an old Beijing custom.**

(Below) **A view of Changan Avenue from Tiananmen Gate.**

(*Left*) **A boulevard in Beijing.**

(*Top right*) **Dazhala, one of the old commercial streets in the capital, the home of business establishments that came into being in the Qing dynasty.**

(*Right*) **The site of a Qing dynasty imperial granary in eastern Beijing.**

teen metres tall and more than one metre in diameter. This gives some indication of the arduous work involved in transporting the huge timbers via the Grand Canal.

At the foot of the West Hills on the western outskirts of Beijing once lay the unrivalled gardens of Yuanmingyuan and Qingyiyuan (the site of the Summer Palace), both built at the height of the Qing dynasty between the 17th and 18th centuries, when the state coffers overflowed with the bounty from the large quantities of grain and articles of tribute sent every year from the richly endowed southern regions.

Yuanmingyuan, completed in 1709 (the 48th year of the reign of Emperor Kangxi), covered an area of 1,330 hectares. With a circumference of ten kilometres, it was one of the biggest royal pleasure resorts of the Qing emperors. It combined both Chinese and European landscaping styles, and borrowed the finest features of gardens from all over China. It was praised in Europe as the "garden of all gardens". Four successive Qing emperors after Emperor Kangxi set up their courts and conducted state affairs from the garden, making it second only to the Forbidden City in political importance. The garden was destroyed by Anglo-French troops during the Second Opium War in 1860, and again in 1900 by allied troops of

the eight powers (Britain, the US, France, Japan, Italy, Russia, Germany and Austria). Its ruins now serve as a reminder of the vandalism of the foreign aggressors.

The Qingyiyuan garden, built during the reign of Emperor Qianlong, was also destroyed by the eight-power allied forces. The Summer Palace was later built on its site by Dowager Empress Ci Xi with the money originally set aside for building a navy. The Kunming Lake there covers 2.6 square kilometres, three-quarters of the total area of the garden. Visitors boating on the lake today might not realise that it was formerly Wengshan Lake, the same lake that Guo Shoujing of the Yuan dynasty surveyed as a water source for the Tonghui Canal.

The ruins of some ancient granaries are still preserved in the area near Chaoyangmen Gate, east of the city. When a number of old granaries were cleared away to make room for the construction of the Beijing Traditional Chinese Medicine Research Institute, the excavators discovered supplies of rice and beans which must have been buried for centuries. Some streets and lanes in Beijing which bear the names of rice, livestock and fruit are the sites of former commercial areas specialising in these commodities in the Ming dynasty. Dongjiaominxiang Street and Xijiaominxiang Street, where many foreign embassies are located, were once called Dongjiangmixiang (East Rice Lane) and Xijiangmixiang (West Rice Lane) because rice from south China was at one time unloaded there.

The Great Wall at Badaling, the Forbidden City, ancient temples and pagodas and gardens in Beijing, the former cave dwellings of Peking man at Zhoukoudian — all these attest to the glories of China's ancient culture, and to the long history of Beijing and the Grand Canal.

But there is also a brand new Beijing. A forest of factory chimneys has emerged in the eastern suburbs to create a new industrial district. Institutions of higher learning and academic research are concentrated in the western and northern suburbs. Everywhere there are new, modern buildings, for

(Left) **Changling, the tomb of Ming Emperor Yongle (1403-1425), founder of the Forbidden City, ranks first among the Ming Tombs in scope and splendour.**

(Below) **Vendors make deep-fried dough cakes at a roadside snack stall.**

the broadcasting and TV networks, post and telecommunications offices, cinemas and theatres, department stores, indoor stadiums, railway stations and airport terminals. High-rise apartment houses stand side by side with traditional one-storey houses around a courtyard. With the expansion of the city, boulevards radiate in all directions, dotted with parks and lawns.

Beijing has recently embarked on an ambitious programme of municipal construction. Under the programme, the capital will not only preserve its time-honoured sites of historical interest, but also become a modern, highly developed metropolis surrounded by satellite towns.

The ruins of Yuanmingyuan, the world's grandest imperial garden in the 17th century, which was later destroyed by foreign invaders.

(Top left) Wooden columns in the main hall of Changling, the tomb of Emperor Yongle. These columns, the largest of which has a diameter of 1.17 metres, were transported from Guangxi, Guizhou and Sichuan via the Grand Canal.

(Left) Kunming Lake (the former Wengshan Lake) in the Summer Palace grounds.

Dezhou

The ancient city of Dezhou, built during the reign of Qinshihuang, the first emperor of the Qin dynasty in the 3rd century B.C., in northern Shandong province, was an important Grand Canal port in the Sui and Tang dynasties (between the seventh and tenth centuries). It became an important gateway to the capital, Beijing, during the Yuan, Ming and Qing dynasties and a major junction of land and water transport between the north and the south. In the southwest of the city was once a decorated archway inscribed with the characters *Jiu Da Tian Qu,* meaning a thoroughfare connecting nine provinces (Shandong, Jiangsu, Anhui, Zhejiang, Jiangxi, Henan, Hubei, Hunan and Sichuan) with the capital, showing the impor-

tant geographical position of Dezhou.

Dezhou was coveted by all the military strategists in the wars of ancient China and became an even more important strategic point after the opening of the Grand Canal. It was from a site near Dezhou that Prince Yan (Zhu Di) waged a military campaign between the years 1399 and 1402 to seize the throne from Emperor Jianwen. Both sides mobilised more than a million troops and transported them and their supplies by way of the Grand Canal. It was Prince Yan's tactic of concentrating his forces and capturing Dezhou to block the northern advance of Emperor Jianwen's troops that won the battle for him, and he finally ascended the throne as Emperor Chengzu of Ming.

Immediately after succeeding to the throne and moving the capital to Beijing,

The tomb of Paduka Pahala, Sultan of Sulu, who died while on a tour of China in 1417, the 15th year of the reign of Ming Emperor Yongle.

(Top left) Stone lotus leaves lead to the terrace where Dong Zhongshu, a well-known writer in the Han dynasty, once did his reading.

(Left) This lake park in Dezhou was developed from one of the old abandoned courses of the Grand Canal.

Emperor Chengzu appointed his minister of construction to take charge of the project to reopen the canal section in Shandong. Some 300,000 builders under the minister's command set up camp at Dezhou and completed a comprehensive project to deepen and widen the southern section of the canal, dredging the Huitong Canal and building the Sinusi water control works at Dezhou.

Over more than 1,200 years of navigation on the Grand Canal, Dezhou grew from a small water and land communications junction into a prosperous industrial and commercial city. During the Ming and Qing dynasties, when large amounts of grain were shipped north, the granaries of Dezhou stored more than 60,000 tons of grain all the year round. Dezhou has been one of the ten largest ports on the Grand Canal since the Yuan dynasty. Over the centuries the heavy land and water traffic brought it a booming prosperity. Local hotels and restaurants did brisk business. In addition to its ordinary markets, Dezhou had special "soldiers' markets" because the Yuan, Ming and Qing rulers all stationed large contingents of troops there. There were also horse, sheep,

cattle, firewood, pot and bowl, silk and cloth markets. Local delicacies such as Dezhou "braised chicken", "street-corner jellied beancurd" and "Shandong cake" are still well known in China today.

A beautiful city, Dezhou boasts many scenic spots and places of historical interest. The abandoned canal channels which crisscrossed the city in ancient times have now become small lakes. The municipal government has built traditional-style bridges across them and turned them into lake parks. Outside the western gate of the city are the Children's Reading Platform where Dong Zhongshu, an eminent writer in the Western Han dynasty (2nd century B.C.), taught his students, and a tablet inscribed with the handwriting of Yan Zhenqing, the famous calligraphist of the Tang dynasty (8th century). The best-known historical site is the tomb of Paduka Pahala, the Sultan of Sulu, in the northeast of the city.

In 1417 (the 15th year of the reign of Yongle), three Sulu sultans, accompanied by a large party of family members and officials, 340 in all, visited China. They travelled to Beijing along the Grand Canal, carrying with them pearls, precious stones, hawksbill turtles and other gifts for the Chinese emperor. The Ming court gave them a warm welcome and reciprocated with gifts of gold, silver, brocade and tea.

As they passed through Dezhou on their way home at the end of the visit, Sultan Paduka Pahala became ill and died. He was buried in Dezhou according to his wishes. Emperor Yongle personally wrote an inscription on the stone tablet for his tomb, gave him the title of *"taiding* (peace) Sultan"*, and sent one of his ministers to preside over a grand funeral befitting a king. Paduka Pahala's wife, his second and third sons and more than eighty attendants remained in Dezhou to look after the tomb. Their descendants prospered and set up a special village, the Beiying village. They adopted Chinese nationality.

Sulu rulers sent officials to Dezhou to pay respects to the late sultan during the Ming and Qing dynasties. A mosque was built beside the tomb during the reign of the Emperor Kangxi (17th century) for the descendants of Sultan Paduka Pahala. Over the centuries, many Chinese writers and poets have called at Dezhou and have written literary works expressing the friendly

Braised chicken has been a Dezhou speciality for 500 years. Meticulously prepared with a variety of condiments, it is known for its crispness, tastiness and lack of greasiness.

(Right) The mosque built in the Qing dynasty for the descendants of those who remained in China to look after the tomb of the late Sultan of Sulu.

(Left) Beancurd is a popular snack on Dezhou street corners.

feelings of the Chinese people for the Philippine people. The Chinese government recently renovated the tomb, and the Philippine government sent its Beijing ambassador to Dezhou to pay homage to the late sultan.

Dezhou, after flourishing for more than a thousand years, went into a period of decline when navigation on the Grand Canal stopped. But it has since grown prosperous again as a junction of the Tianjin-Pukou Railway and the terminal of the new Dezhou-Shijiazhuang Railway, in addition to its position on the Nanyun Canal linking it to Tianjin. The population of Dezhou has increased from 50,000 at the time of the founding of the People's Republic in 1949 to more than 200,000 today. Some 186 machine-building, chemical, textile, edible oil and other plants have sprung up, and the value of their total output has increased more than a hundredfold.

Linqing

Linqing county, in northwest Shandong province, is another region which prospered with the ancient Grand Canal only to suffer a decline in fortunes when the canal became unnavigable. In the early 7th century, during the Sui dynasty, Linqing was an important land-water junction on the northern section of the Y-shaped Grand Canal. In the 13th century, rulers of the Yuan dynasty, in order to dig the I-shaped canal, moved Linqing a distance of fifteen kilometres to its present site to serve as an important inland waterway port.

Not long after the new canal was completed, Linqing became a prefecture. When the transport of grain to the capital reached a peak during the Ming and Qing dynasties, over 200 million kilograms of grain were being shipped to the north annually via Linqing. In addition, local products ranging from tea, sugar, fruits, sesame beans to cotton, silks and satins were also collected there and shipped north. Linqing grew into a large commercial and industrial city. It became the centre in north China of brick and tile-making, cotton textiles, oil extraction and ship repairs.

The brick kilns along the Grand Canal banks extended some twenty kilometres and employed more than 20,000 workers. At night the fires of the kilns were said to light up half the sky. During the reign of Emperor Yongle of the Ming dynasty, court-designated officials were sent to Linqing to supervise the brick-making.

Linqing's grey bricks were of superb quality. They were soaked in tung oil for several months after they were taken out of the kilns. They were perfectly formed, with no cracks. When struck they produced a metallic sound. They were also corrosion-resistant. Buildings constructed of them even in saline-alkali soil remained in good condition after hundreds of years. During the Ming and Qing periods Linqing bricks were used to build the imperial palaces, tombs and temples.

With a peak population of 800,000, Linqing was one of the ten biggest cities along the Grand Canal. Emperor Qianlong of the Qing dynasty, who spent one night there on his southern tour, even composed a poem in praise of the city's prosperity.

The gigantic canal projects between the Yuan and the Qing dynasties have left many historical relics in Linqing. The 100-metre-high Dragon Hill, which extends for several kilometres, was said to have been formed from the earth, stone and sand dug from the canal. The Huitong bridge and the Duzhan Pavilion, built in the Ming dynasty on the site of the old Huitong sluice gate, the memorial archway of the Huitong Canal when it first opened, and the stupa at the place where the Huitong Canal and the Nanyun Canal joined, are all still well preserved. The Linqing Mosque built by General Chang Yuchun, who helped found the Ming dynasty, is currently undergoing renovation.

Linqing's fortunes waned at the end of the 19th century when the Grand Canal was closed to navigation, but over the past three decades it has made rapid progress as a centre of the cotton textile industry, and its brick-making industry is experiencing a revival to meet the needs of China's modernisation drive.

(Right) **Linqing, by the side of the Huitong River, has prospered as a cotton textile centre.**

(Bottom right) **This early 15th century monument was sculpted from mud dug from the bed of the Huitong Canal.**

(Below) **One of Linqing's ancient architectural sites, Aotou Ji (Turtle's Head Rock), stands near the outlet of the Huitong River.**

Bricks from the kilns of Linqing were famed throughout north China from the 14th to the 18th centuries. This dilapidated kiln has been left over from those times.

118

Jining

Jining holds a position of strategic importance in southwestern Shandong province. When Kublai Khan was building the Jizhou Canal in 1278, he ordered the town of Guicheng, a couple of miles away, moved to the canal side. It was later renamed Jining.

Jining had a population of a little over 3,000 when the Yuan dynasty overthrew the Southern Song regime. When the famous Southern Song army general Wen Tianxiang passed through it after his capture, he observed that the place was so desolate that "the streets were empty of pedestrians" and "no smoke floated from the kitchen chimneys". Within decades, however, Jining had grown populous and prosperous as an important stop on the Grand Canal grain transport route. Goods arrived there from all over for processing and transhipment.

In the 15th century, when Emperor Chengzu of the Ming dynasty ascended the throne, he went on an inspection tour of

Jining Harbour marks the starting point of the Jizhou Canal, and is an important cargo-handling depot on the northern section of the Grand Canal.

Jining. Aware of the city's strategic position on the canal, he strengthened its military defences and allocated substantial funds for large-scale construction.

From a fortified village, Jining gradually expanded into a large town with a population of 500,000. High brick walls were erected for defensive purposes, and many luxurious hostelries, restaurants, homes and decorative pavilions were built.

Jining came directly under central government administration after Qing Emperor Qianlong's inspection tour of the south. There were seventy-one government offices in charge of canal affairs, and the governor of the canal was a high-ranking court minister.

At the end of the 19th century the Huitong Canal on the north bank of the Yellow River became so silted up that traffic was impossible, and the city of Jining lost much of its business. However, the less affected Jizhou Canal on the south bank remained open to seasonal navigation, so the

port has continued in use down through the centuries.

Many of the scenic spots in Jining are associated with the Grand Canal. The Taibai Building, for example, was once the home of the great Tang poet Li Bai, who spent twenty-three years there during which he composed around 100 poems. Over the centuries many celebrities, scholars and artists have lived in Jining, leaving behind them a valuable historical heritage.

Many ancient tablets have been collected and displayed in the Taibai Building, including the Zhuangguan (Magnificent Sight) Tablet with an inscription by Li Bai himself. It was discovered during the reign of Emperor Jiajing of the Ming dynasty when the canal was being dredged. The official in charge of the project appended some notes to the tablet before sending it to the Taibai Building. In the meantime, a dozen more tablets from the Han and Wei periods (206 B.C.-A.D. 265) were discovered and added to the Taibai Building's collection. They are among the nation's most valuable relics. Jining also boasts an ancient tablet forest which is highly regarded by scholars and men of letters.

Another historical relic is the Shengyuan

120

Jining's ancient "Forest of Tablets". Men of letters and specialists in bronze and stone tablets of the various dynasties have affirmed it as the grandest in scale along the Grand Canal, with the longest history.

(Right) Yuanguan Lane, one of the oldest streets in Jining, was the busiest part of the city from the 13th to the 19th century.

(Left) Jining is located in the centre of the Grand Canal's lake district, from where water reeds and rushes are collected and shipped to other parts of the country.

(Left) The Taibai Building's collection of tablets includes inscriptions by emperors Yizhong of the Tang dynasty, Hongwu of the Ming dynasty and Qianlong of the Qing dynasty, among others.

(Right) Jining Iron Tower and Shengyuan bell-tower. Boatmen in the old days used the Iron Tower as a navigational aid and the Shengyuan bell as a time signal.

(Below) The Taibai Building, once the home of Li Bai, is now a storehouse of valuable relics.

(Sound Spreading Far) Building, a famous bell-tower built in the 10th century during the Northern Song period. The Yuan dynasty defence minister in charge of the reconstruction of the Jizhou Canal was so impressed with the deep and resonant tone the bell produced that he decided to raise the height of the bell-tower. With the approval of Emperor Kublai Khan the tower was raised to its present height of thirty metres from the original ten metres so that people within a circumference of twenty kilometres could see it and hear its sound.

Every morning ships would set sail at the stroke of the bell, and when dusk fell the bell called them back to the harbour. The light in the tower glittered throughout the night. The Shengyuan Building thus served as both a time signal and a navigation landmark for canal traffic. As it has been well cared for over the centuries, the tower remains in good condition. The bell weighs some 7,000 kilograms and is four metres tall.

Jining has regained some of its prosperity since the founding of the People's Republic, with the completion of the Yanzhou-Jining Railway built in the 1950s as a branch line of the Tianjin-Pukou Railway, and the Jining-Heze Railway completed in 1982. It now has some 250 industrial and mining enterprises employing a work-force of around 60,000. There is even a heavy-duty crane plant which is a joint venture with an American company.

Huaiyin

Built in the Qin dynasty (221-207 B.C.), Huaiyin is the oldest city on the Zhongyun Canal in the northern part of Jiangsu province. According to ancient Chinese custom the south bank of a river is called "yin" and the north "yang'. So the city is called Huaiyin since it is south of the Huaihe River. It has also from time to time been known as Qingjiang because it is the site of the Qingjiang Big Lock on the Grand Canal. Since 1964 the name has again reverted to Qingjiang.

Located at the point where the Grand Canal joins the Huaihe and Yunyan rivers, Huaiyin was a key port on the south-north grain transport route, a salt transfer post and the main commodities trading centre in northern Jiangsu province. Its industry and commerce developed rapidly after the Sui dynasty (7th century) and it enjoyed its best period during the Yuan, Ming and Qing dynasties (from the 13th century to the 19th century).

At Qingjiangpu an administrative office was set up to take charge of water transport affairs, the inspection of passes of all boats plying on the canal and the collection of waterway taxes. Shimatou was the wharf serving both cargo and passenger ships, on which stood a stone tablet bearing four Chinese characters — "Thoroughfare Connecting Nine Provinces". Leading off from the wharf was a five-kilometre-long street with many warehouses scattered along it. Wangjiaying, lying on the northernmost part of the city, was where officials, businessmen, envoys from Southeast Asia and scholars going to the capital to take the imperial examinations boarded ships or changed horses or sedan chairs.

Most of the residents of Wangjiaying ran hostelries, many of them elaborately decorated to attract customers. There were also many Western food restaurants, tea houses and drugstores at Wangjiaying. Along the river banks were chartering markets and inns with sheds for sedan chairs and draught animals. About 100 boats, 1,000 horse carriages, 1,000 sedan chairs and 100 horses or mules were rented out to customers every day. The streets of the city were wide enough for two five-horse carriages to be driven abreast. The total daily income of the hostelries and restaurants came to more than 100,000 taels of silver. They used more than 10,000 kilograms of vegetable oil every day. Practically every boatman, carriage driver, sedan chair carrier and stableman could speak Beijingese (Mandarin) and Cantonese to solve the language barriers between themselves and their customers from different parts of the country. With a population of 540,000, Huaiyin at the time ranked with Yangzhou, Suzhou and Hangzhou as one of the four largest industrial and commercial cities in south China.

Lying on the central section of the Grand

This brick building, known as Qingjiangpu, was a bustling centre of activity for almost a thousand years. It was from here that the government checked the certificates of all ships passing Huaiyin, and levied taxes.

(Right) These old houses date back to the days of prosperity in Huaiyin.

(Below) The ancient city of Huaiyin straddling the Zhongyun Canal. In the late 1950s, when canal traffic was revived, Huaiyin took on a new lease of life as an industrial centre.

Canal, Huaiyin had four large shipyards employing more than 30,000 builders. During the reign of Emperor Yongle, these yards built annually 680 large ships, each with a loading capacity of fifty tons of grain. The imperial court had both a vice-minister of communications and a vice-minister of grain stationed at Huaiyin to supervise the shipbuilding.

The rulers of the feudal dynasties had more administrative offices in Huaiyin than in most other cities to regulate the transport of grain to the capital. They included departments for grain transport, warehouses, river-to-sea transport and sea transport, a general supervisory office, a military office for grain shipment escorts and an advisory office, as well as prefectural and county offices. As if these were not enough, Emperor Kangxi of the Qing dynasty added an office dealing with on-board affairs. All of this official activity only served to illustrate the importance of Huaiyin.

In 1908, with canal traffic suspended, the

administrative offices closed, commerce and industry declined, and many of Huaiyin's inns and restaurants were forced to close their doors. When the Tianjin-Pukou railway line opened in 1911, and foreign businessmen turned to ocean transport, Huaiyin lost even more of its trade. By the 1940s the city had shrunk to 3.5 square kilometres and was inhabited by about 9,000 people.

Since the 1950s the government has put a lot of effort into the redevelopment of water transport on the Grand Canal and the Huaihe River, and great changes have taken place in the city now known as Qingjiang. Today, with the new channel of the Zhongyun Canal still running through the city centre, Qingjiang is once again a major goods distribution centre between south and north China. Using local agricultural and sideline products and mineral resources, the local government has developed light industry, food and chemical plants, and turned Qingjiang into a new industrial town of thirty square kilometres and a population of 160,000. The gross value of its industrial output tops 1,200 million yuan annually.

Sunset over Huaiyin harbour.

(Right) Steamed buns stuffed with crabmeat have always been popular in Huaiyin, and business remains as brisk as ever.

(Left) This ship repair dockyard was once the site of a shipyard built by Emperor Yongle of the Ming dynasty.

Huai'an

Huai'an, home town of the late Premier Zhou Enlai, is situated at the southern end of the Zhongyun Canal. Known as Muokou in ancient times, in the 5th century B.C. it was the terminal of the Hangou Ditch, China's first man-made waterway. It served as an important transfer post on both the Y-shaped Grand Canal during the Sui dynasty and the I-shaped canal in the Yuan dynasty.

For more than a thousand years Huai'an thrived as a waterway communications centre. Foodgrains in transit to the capitals of Luoyang, Xi'an and Kaifeng under the Sui, Tang and Northern Song dynasties, and later to Beijing, the capital during the Yuan, Ming and Qing dynasties, all passed through here on their way north.

From the 5th century B.C. to the 2nd century A.D. Huai'an was but a small riverside town. Construction of the city began in the 4th century during the reign of Emperor Mu of the Eastern Jin dynasty. With the construction of the Grand Canal, Huai'an began to prosper in the 6th century.

Huai'an has been the birthplace of a number of prominent people, such as Han Xin, a military strategist of the Western Han dynasty (206 B.C.-A.D. 24); Mei Cheng and Mei Gao, famous writers in the Han dynasty; Liang Hongyu, a Southern Song heroine; Wu Chengen, author of the classical novel *Pilgrimage to the West* in the Ming dynasty; Guan Tianpei, a national hero during the Qing period; and the contemporary educator Tao Xingzhi. Their former residences, memorial temples and other

The Zhenhuai Building in Huai'an, built in the Northern Song dynasty.

'...al sites are all well pr...
...e city has also won ...
cultural centre. Shi Nai'an wrot...
novel *The Water Margin* after ...
with his family. The Song artis... , a
master at drawing horses, d...   ...ous
painting *In Praise of Song ... nd 35
Other Characters,* based on the characters in
The Water Margin, in Huai'an. He was the
first to make a thorough study of the names
and nicknames of the novel's thirty-six
characters, and successfully portray their
likenesses.

There was also the great playwright Guan
Hanqing, who spent a long time in Huai'an
familiarising himself with the tragic experience of a young woman named Dou E before starting his monumental work *Snow in
Midsummer,* in which he drew a brilliant

characterisation of a brave and unyielding
woman in feudal China. Dou E Lane, named in her memory, still exists in Huai'an.

Liu E, the noted contemporary Chinese
novelist, also spent many years in Huai'an,
writing stories exposing the greed and ruth-
lessness of the Qing officials and other social
evils. The manuscript of *The Travels of Lao
Can,* his most representative work, is now
preserved in the city's Caolou Lane.

Many other famous poets and scholars
down the ages travelled to Huai'an and left
numerous works behind them, such as the
great Tang poets Li Bai, Bai Juyi and Liu
Yuxi, the Song dynasty writers Su Dongpo
and Yang Wanli, and the Yuan calligrapher
and painter Zhao Mengfu.

Over the centuries many historical relics
in Huai'an have been connected with the

The former residence of the late Chinese Premier Zhou Enlai, who was born in Huai'an.

(Right) The graveyard of Wu Chengen, author of the classical Chinese novel *Pilgrimage to the West,* who was also a native of Huai'an.

(Left) Huai'an grain being loaded for shipment to other parts of China.

Grand Canal. For example Han Xin's fishing tower, located at the ancient Hangou Ditch, the Shaohu Lake Park, built on the dried-up bed of the ancient canal, and the Wentong Memorial Tower, built in the Tang dynasty during the dredging of the canal. Other places of interest include the Zhenhuai Building erected under the Song, the big alarm bell set up under the Jin, and the famous writer Wu Chengen's study, *Sheyang Yi*, and his tomb.

Between 1951 and early 1952, about 1.3 million workers were mobilised to dig the 172-kilometre-long irrigation canal in northern Jiangsu province. The canal starts at Lake Hongze and ends in Huai'an, where it joins the Grand Canal and then flows into the Yellow Sea.

This canal helps to regulate the water level of the Grand Canal and irrigates a vast stretch of farmland. And so Huai'an, once a flood-prone area, has today become a new grain belt. Its grain output in 1982 topped 600,000 tons, six times that of the early 1950s. A project to widen and deepen the irrigation canal in northern Jiangsu province was started in Huai'an in October 1982.

Yangzhou

Yangzhou, once a thriving commercial centre, was the first ever port on the Grand Canal, at the juncture of the canal and the north bank of the Yangtze River. It was originally known as Hancheng, and built in the 5th century B.C. by Fuchai, king of the state of Wu in the Spring and Autumn period, between the lower reaches of the Yangtze and the Huaihe River. For 2,400 years the city's fortunes have been closely linked with those of the Grand Canal.

Yangzhou reached its peak in the mid-Tang dynasty in the 8th century. Liu Yan, an official in charge of salt and iron transport at the time, reformed the system so that all foodgrains from the southern provinces would be concentrated in Yangzhou before being transhipped north. Yangzhou thus leapt to prominence as a port for transhipping grain and a major trading centre between north and south. Some 240,000 tons of grain and an even greater volume of other goods were shipped north from the port every year.

The city's economy expanded rapidly, and its shipbuilding industry in particular developed with the growing grain transport industry. Ten official shipyards were set up for building large ships to carry grain and other articles of tribute to the imperial court. There were also private yards capable of building canoes and other small boats, such as dragon boats for racing in the traditional Dragon Boat Festival (the 5th day of the 5th lunar month). One canoe built in the Tang dynasty, and now on display at the Yangzhou Museum, was built of a *nanmu* log fourteen metres long. It was said that Monk Jianzhen in the Tang dynasty sailed east to Japan for the first time in a boat built in Yangzhou.

Yangzhou has always been known for its jade carvings, lacquerware, gold and silver ornaments and other handicrafts. The handicraft industry was already well developed early in the Tang dynasty, when dozens of different articles of tribute were presented to the imperial court, including bronze mirrors and the finest silks and satins in all China.

In the Tang dynasty Yangzhou served as a natural harbour, being only ninety kilometres from the sea. With the development of its commerce, more and more foreign

A stone tablet marking the ruins of Tangcheng City in Shugang, Yangzhou.

(Right) The Stone Tower in the middle of Shita (Stone Tower) Road, known as Yangzhou's "Corridor of Relics", was built in 838 A.D. It has six sides and five storeys, all adorned with Buddha images.

(Left) The ancient city of Yangzhou.

merchants came to do business, and hundreds of ships anchored in the harbour, presenting a spectacular sight. Yangzhou became the most thriving commercial metropolis on earth. Together with Guangzhou, Quanzhou and Jiaozhou it was one of China's four famous international ports, but its favourable location by the Grand Canal gave it an advantage over the other three.

Many foreign missionaries and scholars came to admire Yangzhou. The noted Japanese monk Ennin described the thriving scene at Yangzhou during the Tang dynasty in his *Travel Notes on My Pilgrimage to Tang for Buddhist Scriptures:* "Marketplaces dot a ten-league thoroughfare; when night markets open, a myriad lights glow under the azure sky." This couplet is typical of the poems by countless men of letters describing the prosperity of Yangzhou.

In the late Tang dynasty, Yangzhou suffered badly from the chaos of war. Then, as the Yangtze silted up on its northern banks and its sea outlet kept moving to the east, Yangzhou lost its status as a seaport and as the only transfer post on the canal by the Yangtze. From that time on the famous old city went into gradual decline.

In the northwestern outskirts of Yangzhou was Shugang Mound, where Emperor Yangdi of the Sui dynasty built his "palace city". Later in the Tang dynasty it became the site of government offices. At that time one could see tidemarks on top of the mound. Nothing now remains of Tang dynasty Yangzhou apart from ruins, and the occasional reminder of the prosperous city of old. Broken porcelain unearthed in archaeological excavations of the ruins shows how far-flung were Yangzhou's trading connections. In recent years a large quantity of pottery similar to that found in the Yangzhou ruins has been unearthed in areas around Karatsu and Fukuoka in Japan. It had been shipped to Japan via Yangzhou during the Tang dynasty.

Inside the western gate of Yangzhou is Shita Road, a long corridor of relics — the Stone Pagoda of the Tang dynasty, the Wenchang Pavilion of the Ming dynasty, the Siwang Pavilion of the Song dynasty — and ancient trees. When public works were being built along the road in 1978, a wooden bridge and boat planks, buried five metres underground, were unearthed together with two thirty-one-metre-wide old

A sketch map of Yangzhou as it looked in the Tang dynasty.

(Right) The monument to Marco Polo, west of Yangzhou. He was governor-general of the city for three years.

(Left) The Kaomin Temple, temporary home of Qing Emperor Kangxi, was built in 1703 in the southern suburbs of Yangzhou when the emperor made his fourth southern inspection tour.

courses of the Hangou Ditch that ran through the city in the mid-Tang dynasty. Shopping centres and a ten-league thoroughfare had flanked both sides of the old ditch.

Even when Yangzhou was on the decline, foreign businessmen and scholars still came in an endless stream. On a mound east of the city by the canal was buried Puhaddin, a 16th-generation descendant of the Islamic prophet Mohammed, who did missionary work in Yangzhou during the Southern Song dynasty. Emperor Yongle of the Ming dynasty declared the Moslem's tomb a national treasure. West of the city is a monument to Marco Polo, the world-renowned traveller and merchant from Venice in the 13th century, who served as governor-general of the city for three years under Kublai

Khan, the first emperor of the Yuan dynasty.

Yangzhou is also famous for its scenic rock gardens largely built in the Qing dynasty. It had a well developed salt industry in the reign of Emperor Jiaqing (1796-1820) of the Qing dynasty, and it was as commercially prosperous as Shanghai is today. Yangzhou became a pleasure playground of the rich salt merchants, who built as many as two hundred gardens there. They carried huge multi-coloured rocks home with them in their salt boats for their private gardens. The picturesque Slender West Lake, lined with exotic flowers and trees and dotted with exquisite buildings and pavilions, is still today the most scenic spot in Yangzhou, and attracts many visitors.

Yangzhou was a popular resort for the emperors ever since the opening of the

唐代揚州城池示意圖試稿

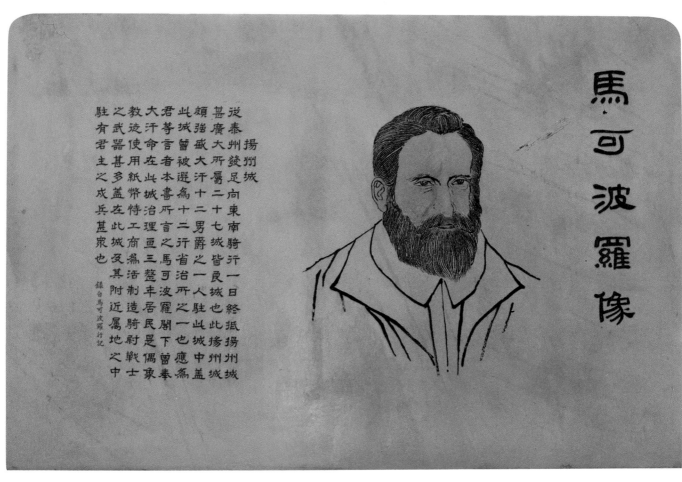

馬可波羅像

north-south Grand Canal in the 7th century. Emperor Yangdi of the Sui dynasty spent a fortune on building the Jiangdu Palace there. His three trips to Yangzhou became valuable source material for the city's unofficial history and popular legends. Emperor Qianlong of the Qing dynasty left his mark all over the city. He built imperial palaces for his short stays, gave grand banquets and travelled from place to place enjoying the beauties of nature. Huaiyang food ranked among China's four great cuisines, and legend has it that Emperor Qianlong had something to do with that. Once, on a visit to Yiyuan Garden, he was fascinated by the beautiful flower beds, so he issued an imperial decree that the finest cooks in Yangzhou should prepare a unique dish modelled after the beds for his imperial banquet. Yiyuan Garden has now disappeared, but the "Yiyuan Flower-Basket Dish" has been handed down since then as a traditional Yangzhou dish.

Yangzhou declined in the late 19th century as the salt trade slackened, the grain traffic stopped, goods transported along the

Yangtze were discharged mainly at Zhenjiang on the southern bank, and the north-south railway was opened. Merchant ships no longer sailed via Yangzhou, and the city's industry and commerce languished. By the 1940s there were only three factories and two schools left in Yangzhou, and the population had dwindled to 100,000.

In 1958, when the Liyun Canal was renovated, the outlet of the Grand Canal to the Yangtze was moved to Liuxu and a new section was dug between Yangzhou and Liuxu to link with the Grand Canal. Since then, Yangzhou has once again become a hub of water and land communications in northern Jiangsu province. A new industrial district has come into being along the ancient canal in the southern outskirts. The urban population has increased to 280,000. Places of historical interest and scenic spots have been renovated, and tourism thrives. A new tourist route from Suzhou to Yangzhou along the ancient Grand Canal has been opened. Tourists can now sail from the canal city of Suzhou east to Yangzhou to admire the unique scenery, to follow in the footsteps of Emperors Yangdi and Qianlong, and to taste the famous Huaiyang food.

137

Jianzhen's Voyages to Japan

A native of Yangzhou, Jianzhen (688-763) was a celebrated monk who dedicated his life to improving cultural relations between China and Japan. He was abbot of the Daming Temple in Yangzhou when Tang dynasty culture was at its height and Yangzhou was experiencing an economic boom.

In 742, the first year of the reign of Emperor Tianbao, at the request of his government, a Japanese monk then studying in China came to the Daming Temple to invite a Chinese monk well versed in Buddhism to travel and teach in Japan. Jianzhen accepted the offer, and prepared to set out for the Land of the Rising Sun with twenty-two disciples. He also selected eighty-five artists, skilled in painting, engraving, embroidering and sculpting Buddha images, to accompany him.

Embarking on a vessel built in a Yangzhou yard, the party set out from the Guazhou Ferry on the Yangtze River. The ship was driven back by storms. Jianzhen at-

tempted the voyage another four times, each time failing. Thirty-six men lost their lives in these attempts. On the fifth voyage the Japanese monk died, and Abbot Jianzhen lost his sight. But no hardships could deter him and in 753, after eleven years of trying, Jianzhen, now totally blind, succeeded in leading his party to Japan at the sixth attempt.

When Jianzhen reached Nara, Japan, he was already 66 years old. He spent the last ten years of his life in Japan, where he taught Buddhism, built temples and cured the sick with herbal medicines he and his disciples had prepared. All these years he worked tirelessly to spread Tang culture, and his contribution to the promotion of cultural exchange between China and Japan was enormous.

When they saw that Jianzhen's health was failing the disciples made a lacquered statue of the aged monk which can still be seen in Japan today, where it is prized as a national treasure. In 1980 Abbot Morimoto of the Toshadai Temple in Nara escorted the statue of Jianzhen back to China for a "visit" to his home town, Yangzhou.

On the 1,200th anniversary of the death of Jianzhen a memorial service for him was held in Yangzhou by Chinese and Japanese Buddhists. In 1973 the Jianzhen Memorial Hall was built in the grounds of the Daming Temple. Its main building, which resembles the one in the Toshadai Temple in Japan, was built on a blueprint drafted by Liang Sicheng, a noted expert in ancient Chinese architecture. On one side of a stone tablet in front of the hall are the characters "Monument to the Great Monk Jianzhen of the Tang Dynasty" written by the late noted scholar Guo Moruo. On the other side is an article on the life of the monk written by Zhao Puchu, president of the Chinese Buddhist Association.

Puhaddin

On the east bank of the Grand Canal at Yangzhou there is a small hill covered with lush green trees. On top of it is an Arabian-style graveyard where Puhaddin, a 16th-generation descendant of the Islamic prophet Mohammed, is buried.

Puhaddin came to China in the 13th century to do missionary work. During the ten years he was in Yangzhou (1265-75) he helped build Xianhe Si (the Crane Mosque), one of China's four famous mosques. The other three are Shizi Si (the Lions' Mosque, also known as Guangta Si) in Guangzhou, Qilin Si (the Chinese Unicorn Mosque) in Quanzhou, Fujian province and Fenghuang Si (the Phoenix Mosque) in Hangzhou, Zhejiang province.

Puhaddin died on a ship which anchored at Yangzhou in 1275 on its way from Jining, Shandong province, where he did missionary work. According to his last wishes his body was buried at the present site, and a graveyard was built accordingly.

Years later, during the Ming and Qing dynasties, several Moslem missionaries who had preached Islam in Yangzhou were all buried near the grave. The hill has since become an Islamic cemetery.

Emperor Yongle of the Ming dynasty proclaimed Puhaddin's tomb a national monument, and decreed that it be protected.

It was rebuilt in 1390. And in 1909, when the graveyard was again restored, a stele with engraved words outlining Puhaddin's missionary work in China was erected there.

Since the founding of the People's Republic of China in 1949, the government has listed the Xianhe Si Mosque and the Tomb of Puhaddin as two major historical sites under state protection, and they are frequently renovated.

(Left) **The Puhaddin Mausoleum, a small but exquisite building of Arabian-sytle architecture.**

(Below) **The completely renovated Crane Mosque in Yangzhou.**

The Slender West Lake, finest of all the scenic spots and historical sites in Yangzhou.

The Slender West Lake

Originally, the Slender West Lake was a river which flowed from the Shugang Mound Springs northwest of Yangzhou city to the Grand Canal. The river was less than ten metres wide, hence the name of the lake.

Its reputation as a beauty spot goes back to Emperor Qianlong's third tour of the south, which took him to Yangzhou. In 1757, before the emperor embarked on the tour, the wealthy salt merchants of Yangzhou dug a canal so that the sovereign could sail from the lake to Shugang Mound, the site of Pingshan Hall, built by the celebrated Song dynasty scholar Ouyang Xiu. The excavated earth was dumped into the centre of the lake to form a hill, named "Little Golden Hill" after a hill in nearby Zhenjiang city on the Yangtze. A terrace for anglers was constructed on a quay jutting out from the man-made hill into the lake. The emperor is believed to have sat on the terrace and fished.

Going to inordinate lengths to please the emperor, the salt merchants stationed men under the water, their heads hidden under broad lotus leaves, breathing through hollow lotus stalks. Emperor Qianlong was delighted to find himself catching fish after fish. Little did he know that they were being attached to his line by these early skin divers.

The story behind the White Pagoda on the lake is even more extraordinary. While sightseeing one day, the emperor pointed in the distance and said to his aide, "How wonderful! It looks like springtime in Beijing's Winter Palace. It's a pity there is no pagoda there."

The emperor was overheard by a salt merchant, who immediately bribed an attending official with 10,000 taels of silver to get him a blueprint of the Winter Palace's pagoda. The merchant thereupon hired a team of masons and had the pagoda built overnight.

Emperor Qianlong was surprised to see the pagoda the next day. Thinking that it was a fake, he went up to touch it and found that it was a solidly built structure. On learning how it was constructed, the emperor exclaimed, "What wealth salt traders have!"

Old Yangzhou was also famous for its Rainbow Bridge, built of wood with crimson railings to span the Slender West Lake in

141

the 17th century. Poets and scholars used to gather there to recite eulogies to the wonderful bridge that arched rainbow-like over the water. Many of their poems have been handed down through the years, and have helped to make the bridge famous across the land.

The most famous gathering at the bridge was in 1658. It was attended by many men of letters and a Yangzhou official, Wang Shizhen, who composed these lines:

Over water the bridge arches,
With railings in crimson colour,
Beneath it boats sail at noon-time,
And over it stroll people in perfumed dresses.

The Rainbow Bridge was destroyed long ago. A multiple-arch concrete bridge was built in its stead in 1972, but it lacks the simplicity and charm of its more illustrious predecessor.

The tomb of Emperor Yangdi in the outskirts of Yangzhou.

(Top left) **Hongqiao (Red Bridge), famous in Huaiyang cuisine, is a culinary depiction of the Slender West Lake's 17th century Rainbow Bridge.**

(Left) **Families enjoy a day out on the Slender West Lake.**

The Three Visits of Emperor Yangdi

Yangguang, or Emperor Yangdi of the Sui dynasty, was one of Chinese history's most notorious tyrants. During his short reign (605-617) he made three visits to the city of Yangzhou — visits which were as much-talked-about as the Grand Canal itself, which was built on his orders.

Emperor Yangdi is supposed to have visited Yangzhou to see Qionghua, a beautiful jade-like flower, but that was just a fiction invented by the author of *The Romance of the Sui and Tang Dynasties*. His real purpose was to indulge himself in the extravagant hedonism of life in Yangzhou at the time.

He made his first visit in the autumn of 605 soon after he ascended the throne. The pomp and ostentation attending that visit was so extreme that he had more than forty temporary palaces built along the Grand Canal for his comfort. He was escorted by a fleet of thousands of boats, stretching end to end for 100 kilometres and towed by 80,000 coolies.

The dragon boat for Emperor Yangdi himself was fifteen metres high and sixty-seven metres long, and all four storeys of the boat were decorated with gold and jade. On the boat were a central hall and an inner hall as well as imperial offices flanking the central hall. There were more than 120 rooms on the second and third floors. His attendants stayed on the first floor. The phoenix boat for his queen, Xiao, was a little smaller but was decorated just as extravagantly. Yangdi was presented with all kinds of delicacies by provincial officials along the route so that he and his entourage could while away their time feasting and sightseeing. When the emperor returned to his capital, Luoyang, in the spring of the following year, there was a lavish royal arrival ceremony with thousands of steeds in attendance.

The Sui emperor made his second visit to Yangzhou in March, 610. By then his Jiangdu Palace at Yangzhou had just been completed. The palace comprised a huge group of imposing buildings, and the tyrant lingered there for nearly a year.

When he set out on his third visit to Yangzhou in July, 616, the country was already seething with peasants' uprisings. Yangdi ordered ruthless suppression of the rebels, but continued his indulgent life. The tyrant and his queen held huge banquets daily for nearly two years, the corruption of his lifestyle only adding fuel to the flames of the rage of the people. Finally, one of his generals, Yuwen Huajie, led tens of thousands of soldiers in revolt and broke into Jiangdu Palace. The tyrant was hanged. The queen and some maidservants used planks to make a crude coffin, and buried the body in the palace compound.

In 622, in the fifth year of the reign of Emperor Wude, Chen Ling, a former Sui official, was appointed governor of Jiangdu (today's Yangzhou). He dug up Yangdi's remains and reburied them in the outskirts of Yangzhou. With the passage of time the grave, which the local people called "the Royal Mound", became overgrown with weeds and forgotten.

It was only in 1809, in the 12th year of the reign of Emperor Jiaqing of the Qing dynasty, that a local scholar named Yuan Yuan discovered the Sui ruler's tomb. He persuaded local officials into cooperating with him in repairing the tomb and erecting a tombstone with the inscription "The Tomb of Sui Yangdi". This was the first time the grave had been specifically marked.

Today the local government regards the tomb as a relic worthy of conservation, and is considering a plan to renovate it so that visitors to Yangzhou will be better informed of the history of the Grand Canal, and of the Sui emperor who had so much to do with its creation.

(Left) **A drawing of the tyrant Emperor Yangdi taken from an ancient book.**

(Below) **The Jubaxian flower of Yangzhou looks much like the legendary Qionghua flower.**

(Right) The labyrinth in Yangzhou where Emperor Yangdi led his life of pleasure, adjacent to the ruins of Tangchen city.

第一靈山

Zhenjiang

Zhenjiang, an ancient city which grew from a riverbank ferry pier, is known as the City of Hills and Forests. Hills surround its eastern, southern and western sides, the Yangtze River flows past it to the north and the Grand Canal meets the Yangtze to the northeast. Three hills — Jinshan, Jiaoshan and Beigushan — stand by the waterways.

Zhenjiang was a Yangtze ferry terminal as far back as the third century B.C. About 600 years later the city of Tiewengcheng emerged, built on Beigushan Hill by Sun Quan, ruler of the kingdom of Wu in the Three Kingdoms period. With the opening of the Jiangnan Canal, the southernmost section of the Grand Canal, in the early 7th century, Zhenjiang became a port on the canal foodgrains route from south China to the imperial capital, and an important distribution centre.

A large silver wine jar unearthed in Zhenjiang in 1982 was found to contain more than 900 pieces of exquisite silverware, all made in the ancient city during the Tang dynasty. The most valuable piece was a tortoise and candle drinking cup used in drinkers' betting games at banquets.

Various kinds of silks and satins and gold and silver vessels produced in Zhenjiang were among the exhibits at a fair displaying articles of tribute from across the country sponsored by Emperor Xuanzong of the Tang dynasty (712-756) in Changan (now Xi'an).

Zhenjiang was at its most prosperous in the Northern Song dynasty (960-1127). Its office in charge of silk weaving presented several thousand bolts of silk gauze to the imperial court every year. More than 300 families specialised in silk production. Zhenjiang silks enjoyed equal popularity with those of Yangzhou and Changzhou in the Song dynasty.

Dashikou, the downtown area of Zhenjiang, was a busy shopping centre in the Song dynasty. A one-kilometre-long ancient street is still preserved at the old ferry north of the city as proof of the prosperity of the time.

Historical sites marking the development of Zhenjiang culture in the Northern Song dynasty can be seen in the thickly-wooded hills. Jinshan in the northwestern part of the city was a place where, according to popular legend, the White Snake fought the monk Fahai and flooded the hill.

The great scientist of the Northern Song dynasty, Shen Kuo (1031-1095) built a house called Mengxiyuan (Garden of the Dreaming Brook) at Jinshan in 1088, and there wrote his monumental work *Sketches and Notes at Mengxi*, described by the noted British scholar Dr Joseph Needham as "a milestone of science in the 11th century".

Mi Fu (1051-1107), founder of the Mi school of mountains-and-waters paintings, dwelt at Jinshan for forty years, where the picturesque woods and hills of Zhenjiang helped him develop his distinctive style of painting. The term City of Hills and Forests originated from his landscape paintings.

Zhenjiang's trading ties were widespread; they reached Shandong in the north and vast areas south of the Yangtze via the Grand Canal, Hunan in the west and Shanghai in the east via the Yangtze River, and as far as Heilongjiang in the north and Guangdong in the south along the coastal waters. Commodities traded included silk, timber,

This tablet, inscribed with the words "A City amid Hills and Forests", is the work of Mi Fu, a well-known Song dynasty artist. It can be seen at the Tablet Gallery on Jiaoshan Hill in Zhenjiang.

(Top right) The Jinshan Temple in Zhenjiang, originally built in the 4th century Eastern Jin dynasty. This is where Lady White Snake's flooding of Jinshan took place in the popular Chinese fairy tale *The Legend of the White Snake*.

(Bottom right) Zhenjiang harbour.

146

tung oil and special goods both from the north and the south. Zhenjiang was the biggest tung oil market in the lower reaches of the Yangtze, and businessmen north and south of the river and along the Grand Canal flocked to buy it. Merchants from Guangzhou and Shantou transported sugar, longan, litchi and other southern commodities to Zhenjiang by sea, and traded them for walnuts, dates, peanuts and other products of the north. They also shipped their goods to Shandong, Henan and some other provinces by way of the Grand Canal. According to the statistics of the Zhenjiang customhouse, the total volume of trade at Zhenjiang in 1907 was more than 35 million taels (about 1.12 million kilograms) of silver.

By the 1920s, as most goods along the Grand Canal were transhipped by rail, Zhenjiang was reduced to a transit port for goods along the Liyun and Jiangnan canals.

Today, following the comprehensive renovation of the Jiangnan Canal, its estuary to the Yangtze has been rebuilt at Jianbi in the eastern part of the city, and a ship lock has been built to regulate the volume of water. This has greatly increased the traffic on the Grand Canal. Jingkouzha, the old exit of the canal to the Yangtze, now presents once again a sight last seen in the Tang dynasty — rows upon rows of bamboo rafts clogging the waterway.

In 1981, construction of a new wharf with berths for ten or more 10,000-ton ships began at Dagang town twenty kilometres away from the city proper to replace the outmoded wharf. The four berths in the first phase of construction will be completed in 1985, when all goods from the six provinces and one municipality along the banks of the Yangtze and from the areas along the Grand Canal will be transhipped in Zhenjiang.

From the summits of the three hills at Zhenjiang, visitors can enjoy a panoramic view of the Yangtze surging east to the sea. Cargo and passenger ships shuttle back and forth on the canal. Brimming with youthful vigour, the ancient city of Zhenjiang will become better known in the world when its new wharf is completed.

(Bottom left) **The tortoise candle, a silver drinking vessel from the Tang dynasty, excavated from the old Grand Canal channel in 1982.**

(Below) **Qing Emperor Qianlong's lodgings in Jiaoshan, Zhenjiang. He stayed here on his third inspection tour in 1762.**

These narrow Song dynasty streets are preserved at the ancient ferry north of Zhenjiang. The stone pagoda that spans the street is from the Yuan dynasty.

(*Following page*) A busy water lane in the west of Suzhou. Emperor Qianlong entered Suzhou by this route on his inspection tours.

Suzhou

Suzhou, the most picturesque city of waterways and gardens in the East, is situated by Lake Taihu on the lower reaches of the Yangtze River. Covering 119 square kilometres and with a population of 670,000, the city, which is square in shape, is turned into a beautiful checkerboard by an intricate web of waterways, streets and alleys.

The checkerboard pattern of the city began to take form 2,500 years ago. Fascinated by the local landscapes, He Lu, father of King Fuchai of the state of Wu in the Spring and Autumn period, started to build what was then called the Grand City of He Lu. Enclosed by a 24-kilometre-long wall of compressed earth, the city had eight road gates and six canal entrances, one of which — the Panmen Gate — still stands today in the southern part of the city.

Suzhou emerged as a bustling port when the Grand Canal was opened to shipping between the Yangtze Valley and north China in the 7th century. It grew in wealth and kept expanding as more and more foodgrains were shipped through the city.

When the celebrated poet Bai Juyi (772-846) became the governor of Suzhou, the city had eight gateways, sixty streets and lanes and no fewer than 300 crimson wooden bridges with railings. The poet-governor penned these lines:

Rivers flow in all directions,
Beneath crimson bridges numbering 300,
Canals run from north to south.

During his tenure in office, the poet-governor had a canal constructed to link the city with the Grand Canal. Named the Qilishantang Canal, it passes through a gate in the city's west wall to Tiger Hill, site of the He Lu Tomb, the premier historical site of Suzhou. With ships coming all the way into the city, Suzhou grew in importance.

The Tang dynasty poet Du Xunhe gave a vivid description of the city in this poem:

Those coming to Gusu (Suzhou),
Find people dwelling on riversides,
Ancient palaces are many with little
 land to spare,
Over canals span bridges in large
 numbers,
Water chestnuts, lotus roots are offered in
 evening markets,
And in spring boats sail laden with silk.

(Right) **Twilight time on a Suzhou water lane.**

(Below) **Fresh vegetables from the rural areas are piled up on the Grand Canal quay in Suzhou.**

Suzhou expanded enormously in size during the 12th century. The city was then the capital of Pingjiang prefecture. On display at the local museum is a stone tablet on which is engraved "The Map of Pingjiang". It was done in 1129, the third year of the reign of Emperor Jianyan. Measuring 276cm in height and 145cm across, the map, the oldest of its kind in China, carries details of the Grand Canal west of the city, the Qilishantang Canal and the Circular Canal around the city. The map shows the web of canals within the city, seven running from north to south and fourteen from east to west — all running parallel to the streets to form an intricate checkerboard. At one spot there are as many as twenty waterways. The map shows there were 414 streets and alleys and 304 bridges in Suzhou at the time. It can be seen that the main shipping and commerce area was in the western section of the city. The city, on the whole, was laid out as it is now. However, Suzhou today has only twenty-four kilometres of canals — much less than it had in Song dynasty days.

The Yangtze Valley became a major producer of foodgrains for the imperial capitals and an important tax collection centre in the centuries following the establishment of the Sui dynasty. More taxes were collected from Suzhou than from anywhere else in China. Grain shipments from Suzhou grew with each succeeding dynasty. The annual autumn tax, which amounted to 20,000 tons of grain in the Song dynasty, soared to 50,000 tons and 180,000 tons in the Yuan and Ming dynasties respectively. In addition many other items were sent as tribute to the sovereigns. In 611 A.D., the second year the Grand Canal was extended to the Yangtze Valley, Suzhou sent large quantities of fish and shrimps to Emperor Sui Yangdi. One shipment consisted of huge jars of fish, each jar holding 400-500 carp caught in Taihu Lake. Another item was a consignment of silvery shrimps which turned bright red in the sun. The one-metre-long white fish that swam in the pool at Xiyuan Garden in Luoyang were hatched from spawn shipped from Suzhou as tribute.

The oranges and tea produced in the Dongting Hills around Taihu Lake were regarded as top-class tributary items in the Tang period. The oranges are still one of the finest varieties in China today, and the tea

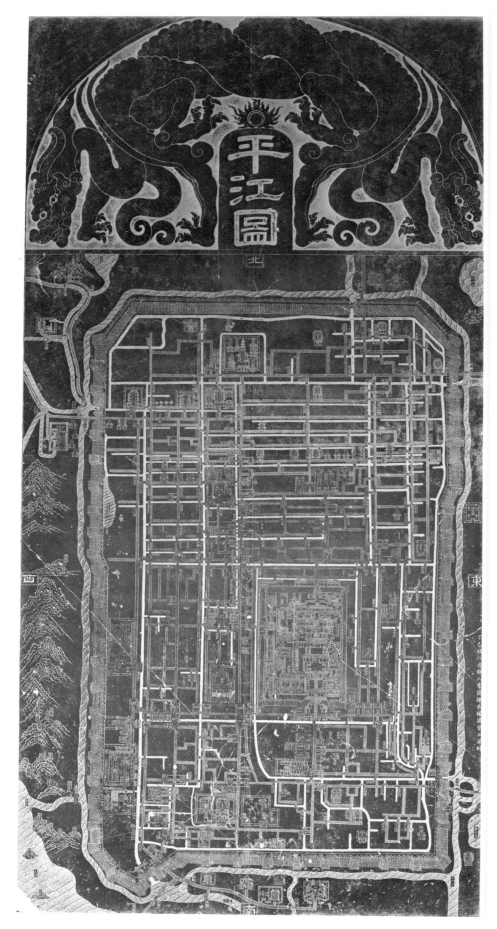

(*Left*) **The Pingjiang Map of Suzhou, the oldest existing city plan in all of China.**

(*Right*) **Most Suzhou households have a canal flowing past their back door, which comes in very useful on wash days.**

(*Below*) **Farm women bring their basketware to market.**

has won a reputation at home and abroad.

With the Grand Canal came irrigation, and an upsurge in agricultural production in the Suzhou area. In the 10th century King Qian Miao of the Kingdom of Wu, who was conscious of agriculture's need for irrigation, organised naval units to dredge the Grand Canal and Taihu Lake. As a result the per-hectare paddy yield in the Suzhou area jumped to 2,700 kilograms — ten times the yield of north China.

Prince Qian Yuanliao, who was in charge of Suzhou's defences, took the opportunity to construct gardens throughout the city. The Canglang Pavilion, the oldest garden in Suzhou today, was built during his time.

At that time Suzhou and the neighbouring city of Hangzhou were known as Su-Hang — a synonym for beauty and wealth. Thus the well-known saying, "Up in the sky is paradise, and down on earth is Su-Hang".

As Suzhou grew in wealth in the Song dynasty, handicraft workshops mushroomed. Streets named after different crafts, such as Embroidery Lane, Towel Street and Drum Alley, still exist to this day. Theatres and eating houses began to appear at this time.

Suzhou emerged as one of southeastern China's major cities in the Ming and Qing dynasties (14th-18th centuries). A silk centre in Ming times, the city boasted many textile workshops, each with 1,000 weavers, and a textile bureau. By 1780 there were a thousand looms manned by ten thousand workers. There were also 76 textile shops, 120 weaving and dyeing workshops, 132 carpenters' shops and 76 gold and silversmiths' shops. Merchants flocked to the city. Traders from Shaoxing in Zhejiang province alone operated no fewer than a hundred tallow stores. There were ninety associations founded by merchants from all over the country.

During his reign, Qing Emperor Qianlong made six tours to the southern part of China, each of which took him to Suzhou. He was fascinated by the city's wealth and intrigued by its unique landscapes. On his return to Beijing, the emperor had a part of Suzhou reconstructed on the lakeside behind Longevity Hill in Qingyiyuan Garden (the present-day Summer Palace). Here a street flanked with teahouses and restaurants was built by the lake, and the emperor named it Suzhou Lane. Qingyiyuan Garden and Suzhou Lane were both destroyed in 1900 by allied forces made up of troops from Britain, the United States, Japan, France and four other powers.

In the Ming and Qing periods, the wealth and scenic beauty of Suzhou attracted large numbers of high officials as well as scholars, who built residences and gardens. As a result more than two hundred gardens

(Right) **The Wangshi Garden, the smallest classical garden in Suzhou, is characterised by a simplicity and neatness typical of Ming architecture.**

(Bottom right) **The Canglang Pavilion, Suzhou's oldest garden.**

(Below) **Chinese wisteria (*Wisteria sinensis*) in full bloom in the Liuyuan Garden. Built in the mid-15th century Ming dynasty, the Liuyuan is one of the four great gardens of China. The others are Zhouzhengyan Garden (Garden of Stupid Politics), also in Suzhou, the Summer Palace in Beijing and the imperial mountain resort in Chengde.**

came into existence. Their exquisite designs and styles of landscape architecture have fascinated visitors from all over the world. A replica of part of the Wangshiyuan Garden is on display at New York's Metropolitan Museum. This was the area where the owner of the garden used to read. It is a perfect combination of the beauty, artistry and simplicity that characterise Ming architecture.

Covering five hectares, Zhouzhengyuan Garden, the biggest in the city, was built in 1522. Together with Liuyuan Garden in the southern section of Suzhou, Beijing's Summer Palace and the Summer Resort in Chengde, it is known as one of the top four parks in China.

One thirty-kilometre section of the ancient Grand Canal that meanders across the Suzhou area is the city's main shipping artery. The wharves in the western and southern part of the city bustle with shipping all year round, and are stacked high with vegetables, grain and cargo of all kinds. Around the wharves are moored hundreds of concrete boats, motor-driven passenger vessels and freighters. Old-style junks with enormous sails are occasionally seen.

The Grand Canal, built to serve the emperors of old, is today at the service of the tourist. Tourist boats make daily runs on the canal between Suzhou and Hangzhou. A newly inaugurated service takes tourists to scenic spots in and around Suzhou before sailing north across the Yangtze to the city of Yangzhou.

One prominent landmark of Suzhou is the ancient pagoda atop Tiger Hill on the banks of the Grand Canal. In a school campus in the eastern part of the city still stands the Ming dynasty textile bureau. The palace where Emperor Qianlong used to stay on his visits is another popular site for visitors. These ancient landmarks give modern man some idea of the grandeur and wealth of Suzhou in ancient times.

Suzhou has become a major light industry centre, but it is still noted for its embroidery, engravings, New Year pictures, fancy fans made of sandalwood and other traditional articles. The city, appropriately, became in 1980 a sister city of Venice, the fading Italian beauty with which it has so much in common. Energetic efforts are now being made to make this city of canals and gardens even more charming and beautiful.

(Right) **The Panmen Gate, sole survivor of the six water gates built during the Spring and Autumn period (770-476 B.C.).**

(Below) **Huqiu Hillock, the symbol of Suzhou, is located where the Grand Canal and the Shantang River meet. King He Lu of the ancient state of Wu is said to be buried here. The seven-storey, eight-sided Huqiu Pagoda was built in the Five Dynasties period (959 A.D.).**

(Following page) **A downtown street scene in Suzhou.**

Strange Rock Chiselled By Angels

Although the Grand Canal was built primarily to carry foodgrains to the imperial capitals of feudal times, it was also used to carry a variety of other cargoes, like the strange-looking rocks that went to decorate the gardens of royal palaces and noblemen's estates.

In the 12th century, Emperor Huizong (1101-1119) designed a rockery capped with a 100-metre peak in the ancient capital of Kaifeng on the northern bank of the Yellow River. An enormous fleet of boats, separated into convoys of ten, was commandeered to bring the rocks and shrubs needed. It was recorded that when the first convoy arrived at Kaifeng, the boats in the rear were still moving up the southern section of the Grand Canal in Jiangsu province on the lower reaches of the Yangtze River.

Some rocks, because of their size and weight, were abandoned by the boats along the canal, and they are known today as "rock relics of the convoys". One such rock can still be seen in Suzhou. Called the Ruiyun (Auspicious Cloud) Peak, it measures 6.26 metres by two metres. The ancients regarded it as "the strangest of strange rocks chiselled by angels". Because it was too big for the small boat, the rock rolled overboard and sank to the bottom of Taihu Lake, where it lay for two centuries until it was salvaged in the early years of the Ming dynasty by a man from Zhejiang province with the surname of Dong. A large number of divers were needed to bring it out of the water.

Dong's daughter later married into one of the wealthy families of Suzhou. The rock was given away as a dowry, and was given pride of place in Liuyuan Garden, which belonged to the bridegroom's father.

This "rock chiselled by angels" left behind by the convoys 800 years ago is still an attraction for tourists and other visitors to Suzhou today.

(Right) **Morning on Suzhou's Qilishantang.**

(Below) **Etching of a typical passenger vessel on the Shantang Canal in ancient Suzhou. With six oars from stem to stern, the boat could move with great speed. Its long, narrow hull was divided into several cabins, each of which could accommodate one passenger.**

(Bottom left) **The Ruiyun Peak in Liuyuan Garden.**

Qilishantang

When the great poet Bai Juyi of the Tang dynasty was governor of Suzhou, he had a 3½-kilometre-long canal named Qilishantang (Seven *Li* Hillside Canal) dug to link the city with the Jiangnan section of the Grand Canal. The street stretching alongside it was its namesake, though it was at first known as Baigong Di (Revered Mr Bai's Embankment) in memory of the poet. Boats carrying grain from nearby Zhejiang province to the capital could take this short cut to the Grand Canal. There are a total of thirteen bridges spanning Qilishantang.

Tiger Tower, the city's emblem, is situated not far from the point where Qilishantang meets the Grand Canal.

Shantang market was a famous commercial centre, with many shops selling antiques and works by noted writers, painters and calligraphers. There were more than fifty temples in the market area during its heyday. Qilishantang was also the home of many scholars and high officials. Rich merchants from the north bought land at high prices and built houses to do business there.

The market was most prosperous during the Ming and Qing periods when trade and industry developed rapidly in Suzhou. Nearly all the seasonal flower fairs and festivals, including the Pure Brightness (5th solar term), the Deities (mid-July), the Mid-Autumn Moon Festival and the annual dragon boat race were held there.

The Shantang Canal was busy with ships and pleasure boats all the year round. It was like a fairyland scene when lantern boats used to take ranking officials or wealthy residents on an evening cruise. The boats were tastefully furnished with satin screens and embroidered curtains, and maids served tea and refreshments throughout the trip. More than a hundred lanterns hung on each boat, with red candles burning inside.

At one time seventeen families in Shantang Street made a living operating more than thirty lantern boats. Some of the big ones, such as the double-decked *Shafei* boat, could entertain dozens of tourists at one time. Others accommodated only three or four passengers. Equipped with double sculls, they sailed fast to suit those who were in a hurry.

When the spectacular dragon boat races took place on the Shantang Canal the street would become a sea of people. Pennants fluttered from the four corners of each boat. Sixteen crewmen were divided into two rows with the punter at their head carrying a

sword in his hand. A handsome lad would sit in each boat to play the part of the dragon prince. The race proceeded to the sound of pipes and flutes, and coils of incense smoke would float out of the temples.

Legend has it that it was at one of these temples that the famous Ming scholar Tang Bohu (1470-1524), who was noted both for his talent in letters and his loose lifestyle, met the pretty maid named Qiuxiang, and fell head over heels in love with her at first sight.

The Bell at Hanshan Si (the Cold Mountain Temple)

The moon goes down, the crow cries,
* cold fills the air;*
Under the Feng bridge, the lantern lights
* prevent sleep;*
Beyond Suzhou is the Hanshan Si;
Through the night the sound of its bell
* comes as far as my boat.*

This poem was written by a Tang poet named Zhang Ji as he was making his way home along the Grand Canal after failing the imperial examination in the capital of Changan (now Xi'an). One night, as the boat lay at anchor at the town of Fengqiao in Suzhou, he heard the bell of the Hanshan Temple. Zhang was so impressed by the sound that he wrote this widely-loved verse. And Hanshan Si was thus immortalised.

The temple was founded in 502, the first year of the Liang dynasty. It is situated between the Jiangcun bridge and the Feng bridge at the town of Fengqiao, Suzhou, on the Grand Canal.

Fengqiao was an important port in the Tang dynasty. There were often dozens of cargo and passenger ships lying at anchor there, and sometimes the flotillas would stretch as long as several kilometres. The streets abounded with shops, teahouses and country fairs, and pilgrims to the Hanshan Si often stayed overnight there.

The bell at Hanshan Si was cast in the 7th century, when Buddhism was most popular in China and it was a common practice to cast huge temple bells.

Hanshan Si (the Temple of the Cold Mountain), by the side of the Grand Canal at Fengqiao, four kilometres west of Suzhou.

(Right) This handwriting of the Tang poem *Nocturnal Mooring Under Fengqiao Bridge* is the work of 80-year-old Fei Xinwo, a well-known left-handed calligrapher.

(Extreme right) The huge bell at the Hanshan Temple, cast in 1906 to replace the stolen Tang dynasty bell.

164

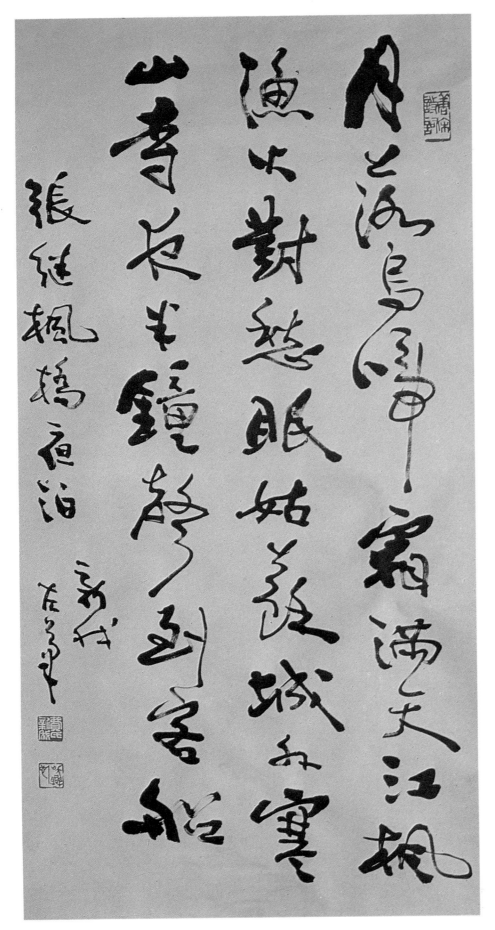

月落烏啼霜滿天
江楓漁火對愁眠
姑蘇城外寒山寺
夜半鐘聲到客船

張繼楓橋夜泊

It was said that when the bell was being made, devout Buddhists gathered to offer their prayers and precious personal belongings. With prayer beads in their hands, they walked around the furnace and dropped their gold or silver ornaments into the molten copper. This made the sound of the bell exceptionally clear and pleasant, and it could be heard far beyond the city.

When Japanese pirates invaded Suzhou in the Ming dynasty Fengqiao was looted and the bell was stolen. In 1905 Japanese Prime Minister Hirobumi Ito made a present of a Tang dynasty-style bronze bell to Hanshan Si. The present bell, however, was cast by the monastery in 1906 during the reign of Emperor Guangxu.

Since 1980 the Suzhou sub-branch of the China International Travel Agency has annually sponsored a New Year party at Hanshan Si. Thousands of Japanese tourists make a special trip to the temple on the occasion every year to hear the bell strike to usher in the New Year. It has since become a popular attraction among tourists travelling on the ancient Grand Canal.

Jiaxing

One of the ten biggest cities along the Grand Canal, Jiaxing is the waterway's northernmost port in Zhejiang province, since ancient times one of China's main grain producers. Jiaxing is a silk textile centre.

The Grand Canal passes through the city, and eight rivers converge here. Made up of more than ten districts, Jiaxing is typical of cities in areas with an abundance of rivers and lakes. A popular saying is that in Jiaxing, "streets run parallel to streams, bridges are built metres apart, houses sit on the water's edge, and people sleep with streams as their pillows".

Jiaxing, which was built in the 2nd century B.C., had a thriving industry and commerce in ancient times. The city is said to have had at that time 100,000 silk-weaving machines and a population of over half a million, of which 100,000, mostly girls and young women, were engaged in weaving and embroidery. By the 1st century B.C., Jiaxing had become a salt trading and transhipment centre. Wu Wangbi of the Han dynasty (206 B.C.-A.D. 220) was the first man to extract salt from the nearby sea. He built up a huge fortune in the trade. After the Grand Canal was dug, many salt traders came from north China to open shops in the city, and spent huge sums of money building gardens. The First National Congress of the Communist Party of China, held in 1921, was brought to a close here on a boat on Nanhu Lake, a leading scenic spot.

Jiaxing was also where the Tuntian System (a system operated by ancient dynasties to encourage peasants or soldiers to reclaim wasteland) was first practised in the country. During the 1st century B.C., a military office in charge of land reclamation was set up here and one of the Tang dynasty emperors even sent a first grade court minister to help settle immigrants coming to reclaim the wasteland. During the Tang and Song dynasties (7th-13th centuries), Jiaxing had earned a good name: "A bumper harvest at Jiaxing means plenty of food for people living in the Yangtze and Huaihe drainage areas." During the period from the 14th to 18th centuries, Jiaxing was known as a place where "grain was transported day and night and the sound of silk-weaving never stopped in every household".

(Right) **The Jiangnan Canal flows through the city of Jiaxing.**

(Below) **Jiaxing was situated on the border between the states of Wu and Yue in the Spring and Autumn period in the 15th century B.C. The southern section of this stone bridge across the boundary river collapsed long ago.**

Jiaxing is still one of China's most important grain-producing and silk-weaving areas. Producing 12,000 tons of natural silk every year, Jiaxing is among the biggest silk-producing cities in the world. The average per-hectare yield of grain in the area is more than fifteen tons. Every summer and autumn when the farmers sell their grain and silk cocoons to the state, the Grand Canal is jammed with boats.

Jiaxing is also one of south China's vital communications hubs. More than seventy regular passenger and cargo ships set sail from here every day. The Shanghai-Hangzhou Railway passes by the city, and highways radiate in all directions. A number of modern silk textile mills and silk blanket factories have been built along the Grand Canal, and the city's unique handicraft — hand-embroidery — has also been further developed.

Xishi, a legendary beauty before the 5th century B.C., allegedly lived here. The house now standing on the site was built in the 12th century.

(Right) The Cangji Temple by the side of the Grand Canal, built in the 15th century in memory of Cangji, founder of the Chinese language.

(Left) Cooked meat stalls on a canal quay in Jiaxing.

(Top left) The Chinese Communist Party held its First Congress on this tourist boat on Jiaxing's Nanhu Lake in 1921.

Hangzhou

The city of Hangzhou, where the Grand Canal terminates, is in the fertile Qiantang River delta by Hangzhou Bay. For more than one thousand years Hangzhou was the starting point for the shipment of foodgrains from southern China north via the Grand Canal to the imperial capitals.

Well known for its beautiful scenery and rich in native products, Hangzhou has long been called a "paradise under heaven", a fairyland on earth.

The city is surrounded by vast expanses of rice fields, mulberry gardens, bamboo forests, fish ponds and tea plantations. In the centre of the city is the West Lake, which makes it all the more beautiful.

One of the famous coastal cities of southeast China, Hangzhou was the capital of the state of Wuyue during the period of the Five Dynasties in the 9th century. Early in the Middle Ages Hangzhou was known as the land of rice and fish, the home of silk, a great tourist attraction and a centre of cultural relics.

The section of the Grand Canal near Hangzhou is particularly wide, with solid embankments on both sides, an indication of how lucrative the grain transport business was in ages past. The Gongchen Bridge, built in the 15th century, was previously the Grand Canal's gateway to the city. It has a 25-metre high arch, high enough for the passage of boats loaded with 300 tons of grain in ancient times and modern ships in the 3,000-ton class. Pleasure boats, passenger ships and old junks and sampans now sail to and fro on the canal. On the banks are shops well stocked with all kinds of goods. Street vendors peddle fruits, vegetables and various local products on the embankments. Their customers include housewives and old folks who like to meet here and lunch at the stalls. This bustling market extends for twenty kilometres to the Desheng Dam.

The city of Hangzhou, flanked by the Grand Canal and the Qiantangjiang River.

(Top right) Gongchen Bridge, the water gateway to Hangzhou, was built in the 15th century. It is one of the oldest bridges in the southern section of the Grand Canal.

(Right) The docks at Hangzhou, southern terminal of the canal.

The Desheng Dam was built in the 15th century as the southern terminal of the Grand Canal. The dam has disappeared with the passage of time, but a bridge standing on the spot is still known as "Desheng Dam". By the left side of the bridge is Wulinmen, formerly an important wharf and now a canal port where more than 200 regular ship services are available daily. It is the main hub of communications between Hangzhou, the capital of Zhejiang, and other parts of the province. Every year four times as much cargo is shipped from Wulinmen by water than is transported by road and rail, and it handles more than five million passengers. Many travellers to Shanghai, Wuxi, Suzhou or Yangzhou choose the canal route over rail or air travel so that they can enjoy the scenery along the ancient canal.

From Wulinmen, visitors enter the city proper of Hangzhou, where the shops are filled with such local products as silk, umbrellas, folding fans, scissors and bamboo or rattanware, all of superb quality and all relatively cheap. The shop assistants are helpful, and can advise the visitor on which products are traditional and which are of modern design. Hangzhou has more restaurants and snack bars than most Chinese cities. They specialise in all kinds of delicacies from land and sea, including such light refreshments as dumplings of glutinous rice, pyramid-shaped dumplings wrapped in reed leaves, and dumpling soup.

From the top of Wulin Hill one has a panoramic view of Hangzhou, nestled around the West Lake with hills on the west and building complexes dotting the landscape on the other three sides. New, high-rise buildings dominate many of the old streets. Although the section of the Grand Canal leading to the West Lake was silted up in the 19th century, there still remains a five-metre-wide old channel and some old tile-roofed houses standing partially in the lake — all that is left of a once bustling scene. South of the city flows the Qiantang

(Right) **A cured meat shop in an old Hangzhou street.**

(Bottom right) **A busy street corner in Hangzhou.**

(Below) **Dragon boat races are held on the Grand Canal outside Hangzhou on the fifth day of the fifth lunar month each year to celebrate the traditional Dragon Boat Festival.**

River, which empties into the nearby sea.

At the foot of the hills the West Lake ripples, calm and gentle as a young lady, the pleasure boats barely disturbing the mirror-like surface of the water. When they held office as governors of Hangzhou, Bai Juyi, the Tang dynasty poet, and Su Dongpo, a famous writer in the Song dynasty, built the Bai Causeway and the Su Causeway, both of which lie on the lake like two silk ribbons. Along the lakeside are the palaces of ancient emperors, built as holiday retreats for their visits away from the imperial capital. There are also a number of high-rise apartment buildings and villas with modern facilities.

The lake has been dredged and widened in the three decades since the People's Republic was established. It now covers an area two hundred times larger than in the 1940s. Many scenic spots and places of historical interest have undergone extensive renovation to look their splendid best.

Hangzhou was the capital of fourteen Chinese emperors. The king of the state of Wuyue built an imperial city wall around Hangzhou in the 10th century with a circumference of seventy kilometres. In the 12th century, emperors of the Southern Song dynasty expanded it to a hundred kilometres and built many pavilions, pagodas, gardens and palaces on the lakeside. When Marco Polo came to Hangzhou in the 13th century, he declared it the world's most beautiful and magnificent city. He wrote that the palaces and stately buildings extended as far as fifteen kilometres from the lakeside. Colourfully painted pleasure boats dotted the lake like stars, and the sound of sweet music was heard day and night.

Hangzhou is now the capital of Zhejiang province. More than one million tourists from all parts of the world visit it every year. Fascinated by its charms, most agree that the age-old description of Hangzhou as a "paradise under heaven" still applies.

(Left) **Hangzhou glitters by the West Lake.**

(Below) **The meeting-place of the Grand Canal and the Qiantangjiang River (top right).**

(Bottom left) **Early spring on the West Lake.**

(Following page) **Farm women come to burn joss sticks in the Linying Temple, a popular Buddhist shrine in Hangzhou.**

Life on the Grand Canal

Meandering across the vast plains of eastern China, the Grand Canal is the world's longest man-made waterway. Dug by the ancients with such simple implements as the hoe and the carrying pole, the canal is studded with scenic spots that have attracted visitors since time immemorial.

The northbound journey on the canal takes the traveller past a panorama of luxuriant mulberry and paddy fields, windmills, stacks of golden grain and sheep and cows grazing on the banks interlaced by gurgling streams and winding paths. The melody of a shepherd boy's flute is heard amid the gabbling of ducks and geese. A boat with a wedding taking place on deck sails past and tiny sampans ply to and fro. The scenes are so enchanting they could have been taken from traditional Chinese paintings.

The women of this area, with their lace headscarves and exquisitely-embroidered aprons and shoes, have been an inspiration to poets and painters down the centuries.

As the ship stops at small towns along the banks, the traveller can stretch his legs ashore and browse among the shops and markets. The shops are stocked with goods from north and south, ranging from sewing needles to wicker baskets and straw mats. In the morning the streets are quiet, but the teahouses are jammed with people, sipping tea and enjoying cakes and delicacies, playing chess or just chatting leisurely. Most of them are elderly farmers from nearby villages who come to sell their produce in the markets and country fairs. Storytellers and singers who speak and sing in the Suzhou dialect are a big attraction in some of the teahouses.

Boat dwellers who ply their craft along the canal have a peculiar lifestyle of their own. As the morning sun gives the water a reddish tint, palls of smoke curl up from the craft as the boat people prepare their breakfast to music from their portable radios. The boatmen go about their tasks barefoot on decks which are as clean as if they were waxed. They wash their clothes in the canal and entertain their guests with aromatic tea.

Unlike their uneducated forefathers whose job it was to carry foodgrains to the imperial court, the boatmen who steer cargo vessels along the Grand Canal today have all been trained in technical schools.

Many junk dwellers live by fishing. Although nets and traps are commonly used,

Morning at a fishing port on Lake Taihu.

179

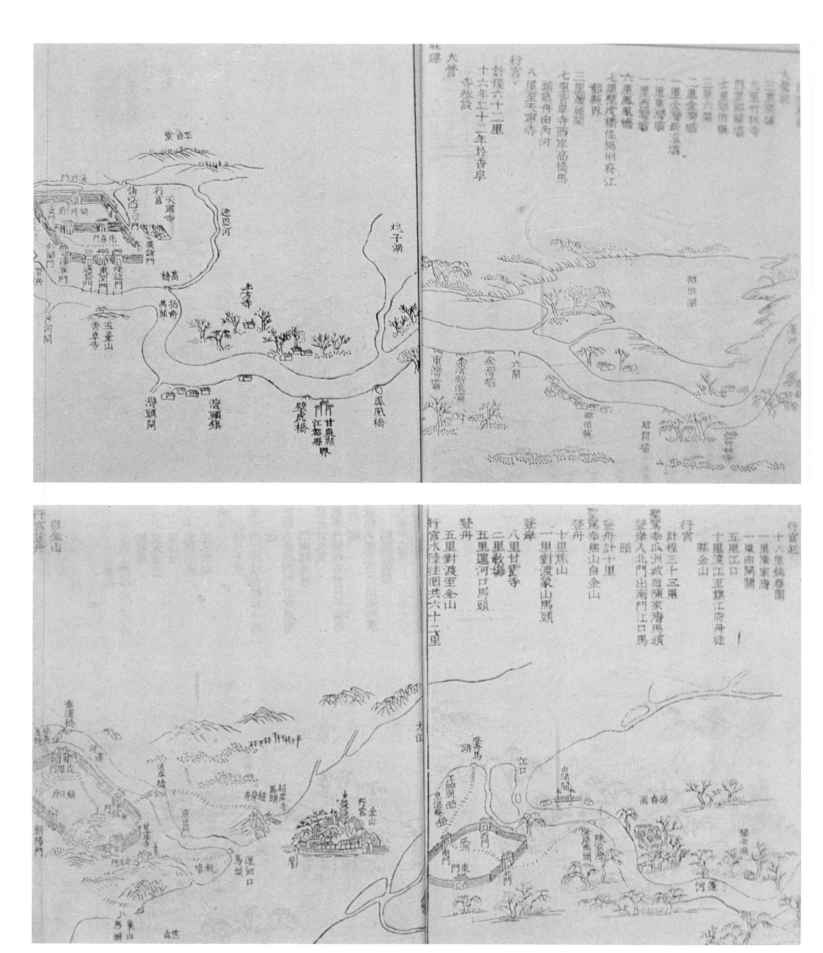

some still fish with cormorants, whose sudden plunging into the water and surfacing with big fish in their hooked bills still delights travellers.

Eels abound in the southern section of the canal, and fishermen catch them by putting basket-like traps at the entrance to the eel holes.

The Grand Canal passes through the lakes of Weishan, Dongping, Hongze and Taihu, all teeming with fish. The Taihu Lake is famous for its whitebaits. Although the tiny silvery fish are less than six centimetres long, the fishermen have to use boats with five to seven masts to net them because no smaller craft can withstand the storms on the lake. The well-known seven-masted boats on the lake were first built in the Southern Song dynasty between the 12th and 13th centuries. It is said that the craft originated from the six-masted ship used by the poet Fan Dacheng (1125-1193) to transport furniture on Taihu Lake.

Fishermen's weddings and funeral services are also held on the boats. When a son marries, the parents have a new boat built for the bridegroom. The centuries-old custom still prevails in which the bride sits alone in the colourfully-decorated cabin as an expression of her willingness to share lifelong weal and woe with her husband in their floating home. When a child is born, the young parents hang up diapers instead of flags over the deck to inform neighbours that a new life has come into the world.

The Grand Canal captivated the emperors throughout the ages. The first emperor of the Sui dynasty (518-618) had a dragon boat built to take him on a two-month voyage along the canal. Emperor Kangxi of the Qing dynasty (1644-1911) and his grandson Qianlong both sailed the canal six times from Beijing to Hangzhou, leaving inscriptions and poems engraved on stone tablets all along the way. Empress Dowager Qianlong returned from her first canal trip with a

(Left, top and bottom) **Part of the itinerary of Emperor Qianlong's six visits south of the Yangtze River.**

(Below) **A spring outing on the banks of the Grand Canal.**

(Left) A portrait of Emperor Qianlong (1711-1799).

(Right) The pleasure boat *Taihu* on the Jiangnan Canal.

(Below) A windmill on the Liyun Canal.

plan to turn the canal into an excursion zone. On her next trip the emperor, to show his filial piety, ordered that the boat carrying his mother be given right of way on the canal.

A trip on the Grand Canal is nowadays considered as obligatory as a visit to the Great Wall. In 1981 a tourist service between Suzhou and Yangzhou was inaugurated. Picking up their passengers at the Hanshan Temple in Suzhou, pleasure boats sail along the same route taken by Marco Polo in bygone days. The 330-kilometre-long voyage takes tourists to such cities as Wuxi, Yixing, Changzhou and Zhenjiang and gives them glimpses of the beautiful landscapes on Taihu Lake and the Yangtze River.

Travellers will be able to sail the entire length of the Grand Canal from Hangzhou to Beijing when the section between the Qiantang River and the canal is reopened.

The interior of the pleasure boat *Taihu.*

(Top right) A boat family's home on the Grand Canal.

(Right) Reed marshes on Lake Hongze.

(Left) A 16-year-old boat girl.

(Top left) A fishpond at Dongting Hill in Taihu Lake.

(Right) Morning chores of a canal wife.

(Left) Taihu Lake — the natural reservoir of the Jiangnan Canal.

A good catch of crabs.

(Top right) Sisters on a boat.

(Right) Drying the nets.

(Left) A canalside fruit vendor.

(Following page) A natural breeding-ground for geese.

189

(Left) **A shipment of bricks makes its way upstream.**

(Right) **A young mother puts her carrying-pole to good use.**

(Below) **A vendor sells tiny silver fish from Taihu Lake.**

(Top left) **Crowds watch the tide rise on the Qiantangjiang River.**

(Right) **Retired boatmen inspect a new tugboat.**

(Left) **Morning market in a small canalside town.**

195

(Left) **Lotus collecting on Weishan Lake.**

(Right) **Playing with a friendly snake.**

(Below) **An old man sells fishing nets in the street.**

(Bottom left) **Stripping maize cobs on the northern section of the canal.**

(Left) **A farm girl wears a necklace of silver.**

(Right) **Farmers pass over a Grand Canal sluice gate.**

(Bottom right) **Paying out a fishing net.**

(Below) **A bride "sitting in the cabin", an old custom among boat people. It shows her resolve to share her bridegroom's life and property, for better or for worse.**

(Top left) A pastoral scene in Yangzhou.

(Right) Storytelling and ballad-singing in the Suzhou dialect, a popular folk art form south of the Yangtze. Emperor Qianlong is said to have spoken highly of the art when he heard it on his visits to Suzhou.

(Left) Washing lotus roots in the canal in Wuxian county, Jiangsu province.

201

(Left) **Traditional dress of the Suzhou women.**

(Right) **Young women go to market.**

(Bottom right) **A boatman's kitchen.**

(Below) **Baby chicks for sale.**

(Following page) **Cherry trees in blossom on Lake Taihu.**

(Left) **Village women around Suzhou cover their heads with colourful kerchiefs.**

(Right) **An elderly couple runs a small store.**

(Bottom, extreme right) **A young family goes visiting.**

(Bottom right) **A bride's dowry is delivered via the canal.**

(Below) **Time for a break in a canalside tea house.**

A fishing village on Lake Taihu.

(Top right) **Fishermen repairing their craft.**

(Top, extreme right) **A young fisherman mends his net.**

(Right) **Loading supplies on the fishing boats.**

(Left) **Children of a fishing village.**

(Top left) **A family of fisherfolk on Lake Taihu.**

(Right) **Multi-masted fishing boats on the lake.**

(Left) **Taihu fishermen delivering fresh silver fish.**

(Left) **Fishing on Lake Dongpinghu in the age-old way.**

(Right) **Setting a trap for the fish.**

(Below) **Waterweeds are used to lure fish into the nets.**

213

Purse netting on Lake Hongze.

(Right) **Gathering fish and shrimp from a trap.**

(Left) **A fish cormorant can catch as much as ten kilogrammes of fish a day.**

(Following page) **Going to the fields by boat.**

(Left) These women are weaving baskets which will be used to catch eels.

(Right) Waiting patiently for his prey.

(Below) Catching crabs by lamplight.

Products of the Canal Region

Silk

China was the first country in the world to begin silkworm breeding and silk weaving. With their dazzling colours, gorgeousness, softness and smoothness, Chinese silks are the stuff of legend. The world's royalty and aristocracy throughout history have clothed themselves in Chinese silks and satins.

China's silk industry goes back as much as 4,000 years. The legendary "Silk Road" was opened in the 2nd century B.C. as a result of the large foreign demand for the fabric. The Yellow River basin was the major silk producing area, with Luoyang (Henan), Dingzhou (Hebei) and Yanzhou (Shandong) the centres in north China before the Middle Ages. Peasant families in the north paid taxes either in grain or in silk. China's rural economy was then characterised by men ploughing and women weaving.

Between the 1st and 5th centuries silkworm breeding and silk weaving were introduced to the south. However, it was not until the 7th and 10th centuries, when the Grand Canal offered cheap water transportation, that silkworm breeders and silk weav-

ers began to pour into the south with their skills and techniques. As mulberry trees and silkworms adapted well to the soil and climate of the south, the silk industry grew rapidly. Beginning in the Tang dynasty, farmers in the south were required to plant mulberry trees and fulfil their silk quotas, and a government department was set up to regulate silk production.

During the Southern Song dynasty, Linan (Hangzhou) became the capital. With the nation's political and economic centre shifted to the south there was a population migration to the region, which further helped the growth of the silk industry.

Between the 12th and 14th centuries silk weaving administrations were established to run large weaving workshops. Those in Suzhou and Hangzhou, two centres of the industry, had a work force of 50,000. During the reign of Emperor Shenzong of the Song dynasty, silk tribute to the imperial court totalled 980,000 bolts. By then Jiangnan (south of the Yangtze River) had replaced the north as the centre of the industry. Farmers on both sides of the southern section of the Grand Canal planted mulberry trees, bred silkworms and employed

The famous Dragon Well in Longjing, Hangzhou, home of Longjing (Dragon Well) tea, considered to be the finest of Chinese teas.

221

full-time weavers. Silks and satins produced there sold well both at home and abroad. In addition to the traditional Silk Road, a "silk waterway" was opened, leading south via the Grand Canal and then to India, the Middle East and Europe by ocean-going ships.

The increasing demand for silk spurred production and the improvement of traditional techniques. Silkworms were bred twice yearly, in spring and autumn, instead of only in spring. Technical innovations resulted in richer varieties of silks and satins.

The silk industry reached a peak of prosperity during Ming and Qing times, but declined in the mid-19th century as the Grand Canal became unnavigable and China entered a period of almost continual warfare between the north and south.

Since the early 1950s China's silk industry has experienced a revival. Traditional products have been restored and modern equipment and facilities adopted.

Suzhou village women in traditional garb.

(Top right) **A Suzhou girl works on a bolt of heavy silk to produce the well-known hand-embroidery.**

(Right) **Silk cocoons are sent to the weaving mills by way of the canal.**

(Left) **A village reeling mill.**

223

Silk brocade, prized as an article of tribute by the emperors of old.

(Top right) This was the site of a silk weaving mill which operated from the 17th to the early 20th century.

(Right) Inside the No. 1 Reeling Mill in Wuxi, which has a well-developed silk fabrics industry.

(Left) Finely woven silk carpets.

(Top left) Gathering the silkworm cocoons in Huzhou.

Two Famous Teas

Of the world's three great beverages, tea, coffee and cocoa, tea is the most popular and boasts the longest history. China is the home of tea. It was used as a medicine in China as early as 4,000 years ago, and by the time of the Qin and Han periods (2,000 years ago) had become a popular drink.

Two famous teas are produced along the Jiangnan Grand Canal — Longjing (Dragon Well) and Biluochun. The former is credited as the king of teas, and the latter the queen. Both were used as articles of tribute to the courts of old.

Longjing tea is produced near Hangzhou, capital of Zhejiang province, where the Grand Canal meets the Qiantang River. The major tea plantations are at Longjing, Shifeng, Wuyunshan, Hupao and Meijiawu, but the varieties at Longjing and Shifeng are of the best quality. Legend has it that a dragon once flew out of a local well, hence the name Longjing, meaning the Dragon Well. The leaves of Longjing are flat, and of the same size and form. Steeped in boiling water, they look like petals in full bloom, and both the water and the leaves turn a clear green. The plantations at Longjing are now open to tourists.

Biluochun is produced on Dongting Hill in Lake Taihu — the biggest "reservoir" of the Jiangnan Grand Canal. Its leaves curl up tightly like dark green snails. There is a layer of soft pale green hair on the leaf surface, and the thicker the hair, the better the quality of the tea. The leaves gradually stretch flat and turn pale yellow when infused, while the water becomes clear green. It tastes sweet and gives out a pleasant aroma. Tourists boating on Lake Taihu frequently berth at the small island and climb Dongting Hill to pay a visit to the tea plantations and talk with the workers there.

Tea drinking spread from the south to the north in the 5th century. Tea cakes were first made during the Tang dynasty. More than a thousand years later the Chinese invented a unique tea-making technique stressing the colour, smell, taste and form of the tea leaves. There are about 500 varieties of tea, which fall into the following five major categories: green, black, compact, Wulong (Black Dragon) and jasmine.

It was no coincidence that Longjing and Biluochun teas both won wide recognition during the Ming period when the Grand Canal was at its busiest. This was because speedy distribution of these two varieties was comparatively easier. Besides, tea traders were eager to send the teas to the imperial court through the canal, hoping that official favour would help their nationwide sales.

Famous teas are the nation's pride. Foreign envoys to China were often treated to, or presented with, tea. When the sultans of Sulu visited China in the 15th century, Longjing and Biluochun were among the gifts the Ming Emperor Yongle gave his guests.

Tea can perform a number of medicinal functions. It helps to stimulate the central nervous system, soften the blood vessels and strengthen the heart. It can also improve sight, relieve fever or inflammation, prevent the decaying of teeth and control hyperthyroidism.

An inveterate tea drinker is said to be less prone to radiation sickness. When the atom bomb was exploded over Hiroshima in 1945, hundreds of thousands of people died of radiation, but many tea drinkers survived.

Girl tea-pickers.

226

A Longjing tea plantation.

Huzhou Writing Brushes

The writing brush was the principal tool of ancient Chinese calligraphers and artists, and the brushes produced in Huzhou were the most renowned of all. But the Huzhou writing brush owed its fame mainly to the Grand Canal, just one example of the role the canal played in developing China's economy and culture.

Huzhou writing brushes are made in the town of Shanlian in Huzhou, Zhejiang province, where the very first writing brushes in history are believed to have been made (by the Qin state General Meng Tian, about three centuries before Christ). The Huzhou brush, however, had to wait 1,700 years, until the first shipment was sent to Beijing via the Grand Canal in the 14th century, before achieving nationwide fame. The emperor and his ministers tried the brushes, and adopted them. They won instant acceptance among scholars, painters and officials first in Beijing and then all over the country. From then on writing brushes became one of Huzhou's major export items.

The bristles of the Huzhou writing brush come from the wool of goats which graze on the banks of the Grand Canal near Huzhou, and the stem from the fine local variety of bamboo. It is believed that only the pure white wool of the Huzhou goats provides an ideal, resilient tip.

Tradition demands that the wool be rinsed with water drawn from the Grand Canal to get rid of the fat and other unwanted substances. No other water source is acceptable. This curious requirement was always regarded as some kind of ancient superstition, but recent chemical analysis has shown that the water in this section of the Grand Canal contains certain properties which help purify the wool.

Shanlian is a small town of 500 families, situated down the canal a little over twenty kilometres southeast of Huzhou city. At one time more than 300 families were involved in the brush trade, with more than 1,500 people making as many as eight million brushes a year.

There are more than 300 different varieties of Huzhou writing brush, falling

(Right) **Many kinds of Huzhou writing brushes on display.**

(Bottom right) **An old writing brush store which has been in business for 300 years.**

(Below) **Young women workers making writing brushes.**

roughly into two categories — the strong tip and the soft tip. Brushes with a soft tip are made of goat's wool and produce soft, graceful strokes. Brushes with strong tips are made from the hair on the backs or tails of rabbits and weasels. But Huzhou's soft-tipped brushes are the most renowned.

The making of a writing brush requires nearly a hundred processes. The goat's wool fibres are not uniform. There are flat, round, straight, short, long, thick and fine wools. Some have sharp ends and some not. The wool has to be soaked, pulled, combed and sorted with great care. A good writing brush is characterised by a sharp tip, evenness of the wool, a plump head and a resilience when in use. These are the four main properties of the Huzhou brush.

Because of the very high level of workmanship that went into Huzhou writing brushes, as their fame spread people began to pour into the small town to learn the skill. By the end of the 19th century about eighty percent of the country's writing brush craftsmen were either from Huzhou or had learned their trade in Huzhou. Subsequently a large number of workshops and stores making or selling Huzhou writing brushes appeared in other areas along the Grand Canal, notably the Shaozhiyan Writing Brush and Ink-stick Store in Hangzhou, the Original Zhouhucheng Writing Brush and Ink-stick Store in Tianjin and the Daitong-xuan Huzhou Writing Brush and Anhui Ink-stick Store in Beijing. All these stores were named after Huzhou master craftsmen.

Girls at work making writing brush heads.

Luoyang was China's peony capital in the Tang dynasty. But since Ming dynasty Empress Wutzetian banished Luoyang peonies in a fit of fury, the Caozhou variety has come to rank first in favour. Caozhou, the present-day Hetze, was on the Grand Canal in Shandong province. These days Hetze attracts artists, poets and tourists from all over the land to see the blossoming peonies in April and May.

(Left) **Zui plums can be kept for long periods**

(Right) **The intoxicating flavour and fragrance of the fruit has made it a favourite for 3,000 years.**

(Below) **Zui plums ripening on the tree.**

Zui Plums

The Zui plum, which grows along the southernmost section of the Grand Canal, is a fine species dating back 3,000 years. Legend has it that Fuchai, the ruler of the state of Wu (220-280), accompanied by his favourite concubine, Xi Si, once made a special trip to the home of the Zui plum to taste the fresh fruit there. Xi Si picked a plum, carefully scratched open a tiny spot with her long fingernail and sucked out all the flesh, leaving only the skin and the pit. This quite pleased her. In her enthusiasm she fondled many more of the fresh plums, leaving her fingernail marks on all of them. Since then it has been believed that plums with such marks were of the best quality.

The Zui plum grows in Zhejiang's Shimen county, through which the Grand Canal passes. The county town was once renamed Zuili Cheng (Home of the Zui Plum) because of the fame of the fruit.

Zui plums are very attractive when they are maturing in early July. They are strikingly red and of a round and slightly flat shape. The flesh is golden yellow and has a flavour that smacks of wine.

It is considered remarkable that such a fine variety should have retained its quality for 3,000 years. The Zui plum is to be found in the writings of almost every historical period in China, the earliest being the *Annals* written in the 5th century B.C. during the Zhou dynasty. A record handed down from the Spring and Autumn period (770-476 B.C.) says that, as Xi Si once became drunk at the town of the Zui plum,

232

the fruit was sometimes known as the "intoxicating plum".

The plum was also described in the *Han Book* compiled in the Han dynasty (221 B.C.-A.D. 24). It was said that Empress Dou of the Tang dynasty also left her fingernail mark on the Zui plum. More poems and essays about the fruit appeared during the Northern Song period. And it was during the Ming dynasty that a comprehensive study of the plum was made with regard to its characteristics, genus, cultivation and preservation, and the result recorded in the book titled *A Manual on the Zui Plum*.

The original home of the Zui plum was the town of Taoyuantou in Tongxiang county, Zhejiang province. Not a single trace of this ancient settlement remains, however. Only the abundant plum gardens survive to remind us of the distant past when Xi Si toured the area and tasted the delicious fruit.

The Zui plum resembles a peach, except that its leaves are somewhat wider. It is about twice the size of an ordinary plum, and should be preserved in special containers. According to the ancient manual, green plums are best kept in wooden containers, half-ripened ones in porcelain or earthen jars, and the ripe in closed bamboo baskets. Most favoured are the half-red, half-yellow ones, which after being stored in porcelain for two or three days acquire an amber lustre and a flesh so tender that the touch of a fingernail leaves a mark on the skin. It is so juicy that one can eat it by sucking, and become intoxicated with its fragrance and taste.

The Zui plum is rich in vitamins B, C and D, phosphorus and iron. It softens the blood vessels, stimulates the heart and improves digestion. The greatest difference between this and other plums lies in the nature of the fruits: the Zui plum has a "hot" nature while the latter are "cold". As a "hot-natured" fruit, one can eat as much of it as one likes, whereas a "cold-natured" fruit will do harm to one's health if one over-indulges.

Since 1949, students and teachers of the horticultural departments of the Beijing Agricultural University, Zhejiang Agricultural University and Hebei University have been doing research on this fruit. With the help of Zhejiang University, local farmers have increased their production of plums, and have developed three new varieties with comparatively higher yields.

Huzhou Dishes

The unique cuisine popularly known as "Huzhou Dishes" takes its raw materials from the aquatic life in the watery area along the southern end of the Grand Canal. It is also sometimes referred to as "Fish Feast".

The famous preparations of Huzhou date back to the Ming dynasty, more than 500 years ago. They boast unique features of colour, fragrance, taste and shape. Known for their light-flavoured crispness, tenderness and tastiness, they represent a distinctively original cuisine in China.

Situated in an area of rivers, ponds and lakes along the western section of the Grand Canal in Zhejiang province close to Taihu Lake, Huzhou boasts 286 different kinds of aquatic life, a record for China, according to the Zhejiang Provincial Research Institute of Aquatic Products.

Consisting mainly of fish, shrimps, crabs, soft and hard-shell tortoises, clams, snails, ducks and geese cooked in a variety of ways, such as stir-frying, quick-frying, sauteeing with gravy, quick boiling, braising, stewing, smoking, roasting, steaming and a combination of frying and sauce stewing, Huzhou dishes fall into three broad categories of cold dishes, hot dishes and assorted dishes of more than a thousand varieties.

The Huzhou chefs can make close to a hundred kinds of dishes with sliced fish only, and their *liu*, or sautees with sauce, are multifarious, with changes in the degree and duration of heating plus different sauces and spices. When Emperor Qianlong of the Qing dynasty in the 18th century visited Zhejiang, Huzhou chefs were brought all the way to Hangzhou to serve him such famous dishes as the "Grape Fish", "Five-Coloured Eel" and "Shrimp-Fish Roll".

At the present time most of the well-known Huzhou chefs are working in the

(Right) **A delicious crab dish.**

(Bottom right) **The "Grape Fish", a one-time favourite on the emperors' banquet tables.**

(Below) **Huzhou chefs prepare their culinary miracles.**

234

Huzhou Restaurant, where the "Hundred-Fish Feasts", two cooking festivals held in 1981 and 1982, attracted thousands of visitors, including chefs and connoisseurs from Hangzhou, Suzhou, Shanghai, Beijing and other parts of China.

The "Grape Fish" dish resembles a newly-picked bunch of grapes, crimson in colour, with scallions serving as leaves. It exudes a pungent, delicious aroma and tastes like a rare combination of tender fish and sweet grapes. The "Five-Coloured Eel" is no less unique. The eels, cut into thin threads according to the different colours of their body, keep their original colours of red, yellow, black, white and purple after the meticulously timed cooking.

The Huzhou dishes are so tasty and refreshing that the notoriously hard-to-please emperors and empresses were forced to marvel at the magic culinary art of the Huzhou chefs.

Suzhou Embroidery

China has four major embroidery schools, located in the cities of Suzhou and Hangzhou and the provinces of Hunan and Guangdong. The gorgeous and elegant Suzhou embroidery has a long history behind it, and a unique style of its own.

The art began early in the 3rd century, and became so popular that between the 10th and 12th centuries many streets were named after it, such as Silk-Thread Lane, Embroidery Lane, Brocade Lane and so on. In the city's outskirts most farming families engaged in silkworm raising, spinning, weaving and embroidery. Suzhou embroidery won an award at the 1915 Panama Fair, and has been internationally renowned ever since.

Since the People's Republic was founded, the Suzhou school has developed more than forty kinds of stitching, and has evolved the technique of embroidering both surfaces of a piece of cloth. The lifelike "cats" done in this way are perhaps the most typical of the products of the Suzhou embroidery school, and are regarded as a Chinese classic.

Suzhou embroidery has been exhibited in more than fifty countries, and Suzhou embroiderers have displayed their skills abroad on many occasions. Embroidered shirts, skirts, handkerchiefs, tablecloths, curtains etc. produced in Suzhou have found a ready market worldwide.

The Golden Triangle of Hang-Jia-Hu

The Hang-Jia-Hu Triangle (Hangzhou, Jiaxing, Huzhou) has been China's most richly-endowed and prosperous region since ancient times. It was therefore regarded as an ideal area to extend the southern section of the Grand Canal.

In the north of Zhejiang province, the "Golden Triangle" stretches from the East Sea coast to the Tianmu Mountains in the west, and from the shore of Lake Taihu in the north to the Qiantang River in the south. It is a fertile alluvial plain drained by the Yangtze and Qiantang rivers. Triangular in shape, it has Hangzhou as its apex and Jiaxing and Huzhou, on the east and west

The "Golden Triangle" of Hangzhou, Jiaxing and Huzhou is an affluent region of rivers and lakes.

(Right) Fishing nets rising and falling at sunset on the Hang-Jia-Hu section of the Grand Canal.

(Left) The beautiful "Golden Delta" region.

(Top left) Silk production has been a key industry in the Hang-Jia-Hu region for more than 1,000 years.

banks of the Grand Canal, as its flanks. The region has been called the Golden Triangle because of its abundant resources, high crop yields and the prosperity of its people.

Stretching 160 kilometres in length and eighty kilometres wide, the region covers 12,800 square kilometres. Though small in size, it is nevertheless a big grain and silk producer. Way back in the Sui and Tang dynasties (6th to 9th centuries), it had an annual output of 300,000 tons of marketable grain and fifty bales of silk and brocade. This accounted for one-third of the total government grain purchases in the Yuan dynasty, equalling the total output of an area of one million square kilometres in the vicinity of the capital.

Its silk sales also made up one-third of the national total. Other products of the region, such as tea, hemp, sugar, bamboo and seafood, also amounted to a significantly high proportion of the national output.

Rivers criss-crossing the canal provide the region with the most developed inland navigation facilities in China. Almost everyone has easy access to the canal. Waterborne freight accounts for eighty percent of the total volume of goods transported.

Since the founding of New China, the region has seen considerable progress in agricultural and industrial production. Early in the 1960s, the annual grain output per *mu* (15 *mu* to a hectare) already topped one ton, and silk production was the highest in the whole country. Huzhou alone produced 15,000 tons of silk to become the world's number one silk producing city. A number of modern factories making silk fabrics have sprung up along the canal. The region is noted for its typically oriental embroidery.

With its rich natural resources, beautiful landscapes and good transport facilities, the Golden Triangle attracts many tourists, currently more than two million a year.

(Right) **The Golden Triangle is rich in rapeseed, one of China's oil-bearing crops.**

(Bottom right) **Geese and ducks are bred throughout the Triangle.**

(Below) **A fish-breeding research institute in the Golden Triangle.**

Sailing boats are still an important means of transport in the Hang-Jia-Hu Triangle.

(Top right) A fish market.

(Right) High-yield tomatoes. In the Triangle one hectare can produce 25 tons.

(Left) A primitive means of fishing.

A total of 13,000 bridges span the waterways of the Hangzhou-Jiaxing-Huzhou region.

(Right) Thick, tall, green bamboos add to the beauty of the region.

(Left) Feather fans made in Huzhou have a long history, and enjoy good sales abroad.

Yangzhou Jade Carving

Held in high repute among oriental arts, Chinese jade carving turns fine, hard stones of natural coloration into figures, flowers, birds, animals, vases and incense burners. Jade carvings are collected for aesthetic pleasure: they are studied, treasured and used as decorations.

One jade *cong* (a jade container for sacrificial offerings) unearthed from an ancient tomb in the lower reaches of the Yangtze River was estimated to be 4,000 years old, proving that jade carving was one of China's most ancient arts.

During the Tang dynasty jade carving was a popular pursuit in Yangzhou. The craftsmen who accompanied the monk Jianzhen when he sailed to Japan were all from Yangzhou. The craft thrived during the Ming and Qing dynasties, and Yangzhou became the centre of the trade. One huge piece entitled *The Great Yu Subdues the Flood*, on display in the Palace Museum in Beijing, was carved by Yangzhou craftsmen during the Ming period. The original white stone, which weighed several tons, was found in Xinjiang and transported to Yangzhou along the Grand Canal. The Yangzhou craftsmen studied it carefully before taking six long years to carve it. The imposing design reflects the scope of the arduous undertaking. When completed, the carving was transported to Beijing, again via the canal. It weighs some 5,300 kilograms.

Today, the Yangzhou jade craftsmen produce not only elaborate carvings of classical subjects with intricate, elegant designs, but also small, simple ones, such as figures and horses, to satisfy the growing needs of tourism.

(Right) **Earthenware teapots produced in Yixiang are favourites of tea drinkers everywhere.**

(Below) **Woodcutter Fu Yejin has pursued the art of making woodcut new year pictures for more than forty years.**

244

Taohuawu Woodcut New Year Pictures

Taohuawu in Suzhou, in the south, and Yangliuqing in Tianjin, in the north, are China's twin centres of woodcut new year pictures.

Taohuawu woodcut new year pictures are not only popular among Chinese. They are also exhibited in many European art galleries and museums, where they are prized for their dazzling colours and bold prints, rich flavour of life and fitness for ornamentation.

The Taohuawu woodcut new year picture originated in the Ming dynasty and flourished between the reigns of Emperors Yongzheng and Qianlong (1723-1796) in the Qing dynasty. At that time in Taohuawu there were more than forty shops and printworks geared to the production of the pictures. Most of these pictures portrayed life in Suzhou during Emperor Qianlong's reign. One picture handed down from the period shows a stage performance of the *pingtan*, the local Suzhou ballad, sung to the accompaniment of the traditional Chinese string instrument, the *pipa*. With simple but vivid strokes, the picture recreates the scene of a *pingtan* show at the private residence of a rich family in the Qing dynasty.

A woodcut new year picture — *Emperor Suiyang visits South China.*

Changzhou combs were famous as long ago as the Eastern Han dynasty.

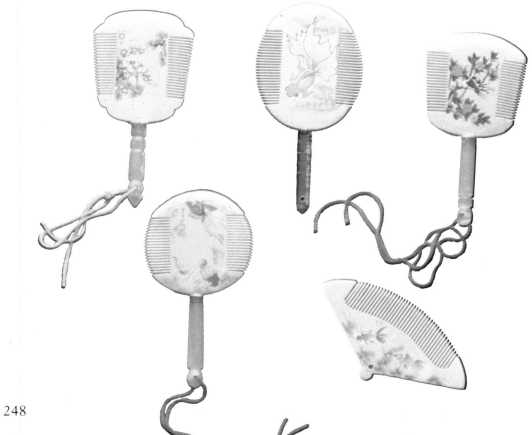

An artist hand-paints a folding fan in Hangzhou.

(Top right) Fans from Huzhou.

(Right) Wuxi ceramics have a history of 400 years.

(Left) Comb-fans from Suzhou.

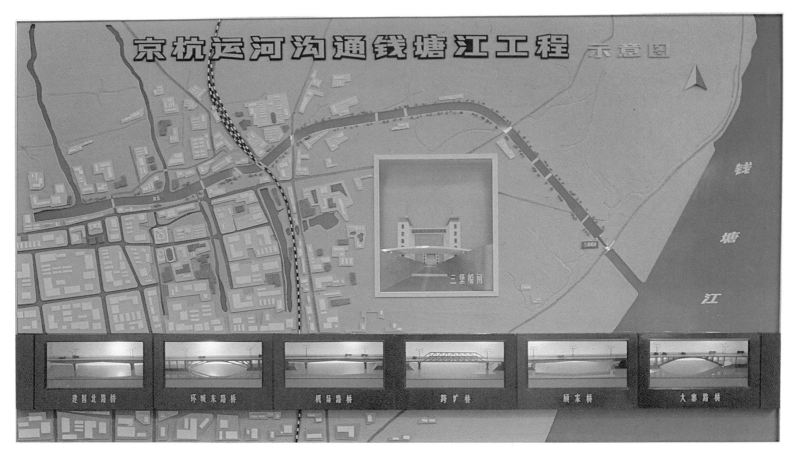

Water Control Projects

(Above) A map of the project connecting the Grand Canal with the Qiantang River.

(Right) The Huai'an Water Control Project — a two-stage intake system to divert water from the south to the north.

(Left) The No. 2 Water Pumping Station in Huai'an.